Crying for Justice

Crying for Justice

What the PSALMS teach us about
MERCY and VENGEANCE in an age of TERRORISM

John N. Day

Inter-Varsity Press

Crying for Justice: What the Psalms Teach Us About Mercy and Vengeance in an Age of Terrorism

© 2005 by John N. Day

Published by Kregel Publications, a division of Kregel, Inc., P.O. Box 2607, Grand Rapids, MI 49501

and by Inter-Varsity Press, 38 De Montfort Street, Leicester, LE1 7GP, England; email: ivp@ivp-editorial.co.uk; Web site: www.ivpbooks.com.

Unless otherwise noted, the translations of Scripture throughout this work are the author's own.

Unless otherwise noted, all Old Testament quotations conform to Hebrew Bible numbering.

Scripture quotations marked NIV are from the *Holy Bible: New International Version*®. Copyright © 1973, 1978, 1984 by the International Bible Society. Used by permission of Zondervan Publishing House. All rights reserved.

US ISBN 0-8254-2446-1

British Library Cataloguing in Publication Data
A catalogue record for this book is available from the British Library
UK ISBN-13: 978-1-84474-108-3
UK ISBN-10: 1-84474-108-7

Printed in the United States of America

05 06 07 08 09 / 5 4 3 2 1

To my beloved wife, Lorri—
"the image of beauty; a heart that beats for God."

Contents

Facing the Problem

The world changed on that morning. On September 11, 2001, airliners slammed into the World Trade Center in New York City and into the Pentagon in Washington, D.C. Westerners suddenly felt a stunning vulnerability, realizing that a dedicated enemy can take thousands of lives in a moment.

Christians in particular feel more exposed. Hostility toward people of faith has become more overt in the post-Christian atmosphere of Europe and North America, where Christians have always assumed that they would have a safe haven. The Internet and mass media, too, bring Western Christians into closer identification with believers in parts of the world where enmity against Christianity is long-standing. But Western Christians have seldom had to stare stark, violent hatred in the face. This experience should encourage thoughtful discussion about the characteristic Christian response of love and kindness.

The question is whether the biblical response has nuance beyond the traditional Christian "love ethic." Individuals, organizations, and governments target the people of God with extreme antipathy and brutality. Does the response of faith never extend past the admonition to "turn the other cheek"? In situations where people stand with such evil intent against God and his people, what is the Christian response to be? Is there ever "a time to curse"?[1]

Biblical examples of another response, dark and disturbing and uncomfortable, do appear. Incredibly, this response is most evident in

Psalms, for millennia the song and prayer book of Christians and Jews. The book of Psalms reveals startling poetic invocations of *imprecation*—curses and cries for vengeance.[2] There is hardly an area of biblical theology more troublesome to the Christian conscience than the so-called *imprecatory psalms*—psalms that declare a desire for God's just vengeance to fall upon enemies. They naturally evoke a reaction of revulsion in Christians schooled in the "law of Christ."

The imprecatory psalms particularly trouble those who view these "curses" as the very Word of God. In the West, where the arm of persecution is still relatively short, the venom in these psalms scrapes abrasively against the modern reader's sweeter sensibilities. Aren't followers of Christ called to "love our enemies" (Matt. 5:44), to "bless and curse not" (Rom. 12:14)? How, then, can Scripture justly call for the barbaric "dashing of infants" (Ps. 137:9), the "bathing of feet in the blood of the wicked" (58:10), or the cursing of future generations in an offender's family (109:10–15)?[3]

Are imprecatory psalms merely a way of venting rage without really meaning it? Or is cursing enemies the "Old Testament way," while loving enemies is a different "New Testament way"? Has the morality of Scripture evolved? And is it legitimate to use these psalms in Christian life and worship?

A few modern treatments can be found of the imprecatory psalms and the problem of their relation to biblical theology and to what is in some circles called the "New Testament believer." These treatments, however, have been, in large measure, cursory, and the proposed solutions have been largely inadequate theologically.[4] The imprecatory psalms have been unsatisfactorily explained in three ways: (1) as evil emotions—whether to be suppressed or expressed;[5] (2) an old covenant morality inconsistent with the new covenant church;[6] (3) words appropriately uttered solely from the lips of Christ and consequently uttered only by his followers through him and his cross.[7]

In contrast, I propose to recover the proper use of the imprecatory psalms for the New Testament church. First, these psalms root their theology of cursing in Torah. Authorization to cry out for God's vengeance is strongly set out in the Song of Moses (Deut. 32), the *lex talionis* (e.g., Deut. 19), and the covenant of God with his people (e.g., Gen. 12). Second, this theology is carried through essentially unchanged to the end of the New Testament canon (e.g., Rev. 6:10; 18:20), buttressing its applicability to believers today. Some Old Testament and New Testament passages appear to contradict the cry of the imprecatory psalms, but texts throughout Scripture also confirm the right of God's people to plead for justice.

"Loving" and "cursing" are kept in harmonic tension throughout Scripture so that in every era of their lives God's people must wrestle with the implications of both in their context. Since the character of God does not change, the essence of his ethical requirements does not change. Therefore, as the imprecatory psalms were at times appropriate on the lips of believers before the Incarnation, so they—or their like—are at times appropriate on the lips of believers today. There is a time and place to call for tangible, temporal divine judgment; there is, indeed, a "time to curse."

The Time for Justice

The Stigma of Vengeance

The central issue of divine vengeance presents an initial stigma. This is so partly because the promise of divine vengeance forms much of the basis upon which the psalmists voice their cries of cursing and partly because of the concept of vengeance itself. To the modern ear, the word *vengeance* evokes images of malice and revenge. By its very nature it bears negative, even sinful connotations. In this mind-set, vengeance—whether human or divine—is in no sense to be construed as virtuous. But to the ancient Israelite and through the pages of Scripture, the concept of *vengeance* is tied to the requirements of justice.[8] Where justice is trampled, vengeance is demanded.[9] The display of God's vengeance, as presented in Scripture, is, in fact, coupled with his character as just and holy and his claim as world sovereign.[10] Indeed, the Scriptures do not equivocate in their proclamation of Yahweh not only as Warrior, but also as Judge and King. As H. G. L. Peels observes,

> If it is said of this God, who is King, that he avenges himself, this can no longer be considered to be indicative of an evil humor, a

tyrannical capriciousness, or an eruption of rancor. God's vengeance is kingly vengeance. If he takes vengeance, he does so as the highest authority exercising punishing justice. The vengeance of God is the action of God-as-King in the realization of his sovereign rule. This action is directed against those who offend God's majesty through transgression against his honor, his justice or his people.[11]

Furthermore, God's vengeance is inseparably linked to his lovingkindness.[12] His vengeance is the other side of his compassion, the "dark side" of his mercy.[13] The Scriptures are definite in affirming that God is by no means an indifferent Being but one who in history has passionately and decisively taken sides *for* his people.[14] If he is to save his people from sin, oppression, and injustice, he must exact vengeance upon his enemies—the enemies of his people.

This understanding of divine vengeance is borne out, for example, by Yahweh's execution of vengeance against Edom.[15] In the book of Isaiah, the language of vengeance is the language of violence—of slaughter and sacrifice, of holy war[16] and jealous rage.[17] As a consequence, the imagery of vengeance is the gruesome imagery of gore: "Yahweh's sword is all bloody, it is gorged with fat" (Isa. 34:6). However, lest Yahweh become relegated to the company of pagan and bloodthirsty deities, notice in Isaiah the stated purpose of this violence against the wicked: "to contend for Zion" (34:8). This point is reiterated in the next chapter of Isaiah, which speaks of the paradise of the redeemed arising out of the carnage against the wicked: "Behold, your God, *he will come with vengeance;* with divine recompense he will come, *and he will save you*" (Isa. 35:4; cf. 63:3–4, emphasis added). Yahweh is a God who saves his people; but without God's vengeance *against* his enemies, there can be no salvation *for* his people.

The ramifications of this tension are weighty. Raymond Swartzbach goes so far as to assert that, without a clear understanding of the significance of divine vengeance, "there is no way of comprehending the nature of the Christian God, for we can never speak of the 'love' and 'justice' of God without reflecting upon his 'wrath' and 'vengeance.'"[18] Hans-Joachim Kraus echoes this point:

The "vengeance" for which Israel hopes is God's judgment in response to the scorn and mockery of the enemy nations. The prayer is that Yahweh will not allow his enemies free rein or let their rage go unanswered. It is expected that Yahweh will manifest his power in the world of the nations. Not alone in the Old Testament, but in the New Testament as well, there is a certainty that this will not take place in an invisible, ideal realm of retribution, but in the reality of this world. Therefore there rings out a cry for revenge and for God's judgment in the face of the unbearable suffering and torment of God's people, on down to the Revelation of John (6:10). To set up a polarity of love and vengeance would involve a total misunderstanding of biblical truth.[19]

But the question may yet be asked, *How can it be right for Christians to cry out for divine vengeance and violence, as in the imprecatory psalms?* Four observations from Scripture address this question.

First, the vengeance appealed for is not personally enacted. Rather, God is called upon to be the Avenger.

Second, this appeal is based upon the covenant promises of God,[20] most notable of which are "He who curses you, I will curse" (Gen. 12:3), and "Vengeance is Mine, I will repay" (Deut. 32:35). If God has so promised, then it would not seem wrong for his people to petition him (even passionately) to fulfill these promises.[21]

Third, both testaments record examples of God's people on earth calling down curses or crying for vengeance. Yet there is no literary or theological intimation of divine disapproval over such sentiments being expressed. Indeed, the implication is that, in its appropriate place, such utterances are commendable (cf. the imprecatory psalms and the Pauline and Petrine curses of Gal. 1:8–9 and Acts 8:20).

Fourth, Scripture further records an instance in which God's people in heaven, where there is no sin, cry out for divine vengeance and are comforted by the assurance of its impending enactment (Rev. 6:9–11). Since these martyred saints are perfected, their entreaty would presumably be "right."

Extreme Ethics

Thus, whereas "love and blessing" is the *characteristic ethic* of the believer throughout Scripture, "cursing and calling for divine vengeance" is the believer's *extreme ethic*—legitimately used in extreme circumstances against the hardened deceitful, violent, immoral, and unjust. Although Christians must continually seek reconciliation and practice long-suffering, forgiveness, and kindness (after the pattern of God),[22] there comes a point at which justice must be enacted—whether from God directly (Rom. 12:19[23]) or through his representatives (in particular, the state and its judicial system—Rom. 13:4[24]).

Indeed, when examining the patterns of God, Christ, and God's people in the Scriptures, this dual response toward enmity emerges—the one reaction *characteristic* of the divine and Christian life, and the other exhibited in *extreme* instances.

The pattern of God's actions in Scripture is characterized by long-suffering grace. But then comes the point of judgment. The inhabitants of Canaan experienced this extended grace followed by decisive judgment when, after four hundred years, their "iniquity became complete" (cf. Gen. 15:16). Likewise, the Israelites of the Exodus, after repeated rebellion and unbelief, were finally barred from the Promised Land (cf. Num. 14).[25] The generation of the Exile found out what life was like when, after two hundred years of God's patience, his hand of grace was released and justice was given her due (cf. Hosea).[26] There is long-suffering to God's grace, but there is also judgment. Note the balance between the two in that supreme revelation of the character of God in Exodus 34:6–7.[27]

The pattern of Christ is also that of repeated grace, but then comes the point of judgment.[28] In the closing chapters of the Bible, both God and Christ are revealed as the Divine Avenger (Rev. 6:9–17; 18:21–19:2; 19:11–16). After the grapes are trampled in the bloody winepress of God's wrath (Rev. 14:19–20),[29] the saints in heaven sing the "Song of Moses" and the "Song of the Lamb" (Rev. 15:3–4).[30] The same Christ who said, "Love your enemies," will return one day in vengeance to destroy the recalcitrant.

So also the pattern of God's people is to be that of repeated grace. But there may also come a point in time when judgment must be called for (i.e., the voicing of imprecations), and the righteous will delight to see it accomplished (e.g., Ps. 58:10–11; Rev. 18:20).

Addressing the Issue

Heightened Need

The current climate of terrorism and the continued presence of persecution against the church cannot be denied. Yet the church tends to shy away from any "real" application of imprecation. Thus arises an intensified need for a reasoned biblical defense of the appropriate use of imprecation within the context of Christian ethics. Indeed, the startling events of September 11, 2001, introduced an era marked by a heightened awareness of severe enmity.

What should be the Christian response to such enmity? The answer to this polarizing question is at once uncomfortable, controversial, and transformational. Raymond Surburg reflects,

> When all is quiet and peaceful in the Church, many may not feel very keenly the need for the use of the Imprecatory Psalms. . . . However, when persecution bursts upon the Church, as has been the case in communistic and atheistic Russia, in Communist China, in Cuba where Christian pastors and their flocks have been subjected to torture, inhuman indignities and death, when the faith of God's people is severely tried by the enemies of the Lord, Christians have instinctively turned to these psalms. Some people may have considered the Imprecatory Psalms an offense in better days, but their relevancy has been brought home to them, when the forces of evil have persecuted and tortured them because of belief in God and faith in the Lordship of Jesus Christ.[31]

Method of Approach

This current study establishes a proposition: *In circumstances of sustained injustice, hardened enmity, and gross oppression, it has always been appropriate for a believer to utter imprecations against enemies or to appeal for the onslaught of divine vengeance. In certain instances today, appeals to God for his curse or vengeance are fitting.*

And while this current work sustains that the sentiment expressed in the imprecatory psalms is consistent with the ethics of all Scripture, it readily recognizes that the New Testament shows a certain progress in the outworking of that essentially equivalent ethic. Between these psalms and the New Testament ethic there exists, indeed, a degree of difference in emphasis. In the New Testament, less stress is placed on imprecation and the enactment of temporal judgments, while more frequent and explicit calls are made for kindness in anticipation of the eschatological judgment.[32] Such difference in emphasis is to be expected, for the new era is the age of "grace upon grace" (John 1:16), inaugurated in the coming of Christ. Again, however, the difference is in degree, rather than in kind. For in regard to evil, the tension continues in the New Testament between the characteristic ethic and the extreme ethic of the Christian. And the New Testament still finds a legitimate place for imprecation, based upon the same elements that serve to justify the imprecations in the Psalms.

Psalms that contain an expression of curse or desire for divine vengeance are quite numerous, covering some ninety-eight verses in thirty-two psalms.[33] The problem of the imprecatory psalms and their relation to Christian ethics is, therefore, addressed by looking primarily at three psalms. Each represents one of the three spheres of cursing found within the larger corpus of imprecatory psalms:

- Psalm 58—imprecation against a societal enemy;
- Psalm 137—imprecation against a national or community enemy;
- Psalm 109—imprecation against a personal enemy.

All the other imprecatory psalms find their lodging in the shade of these three and will be dealt with only secondarily.[34] These three psalms are chosen specifically because they contain the harshest language or most severe imprecations against the enemies. If, then, an answer may be given to these, then an answer may be given to all.

Three Groups of Imprecatory Psalms

1. Imprecation Against Societal Enemy: 58; 94
2. Imprecation Against Nation or Community: 68; 74; 79; 83; 129; 137
3. Imprecation Against Personal Enemy: 5; 6; 7; 9; 10; 17; 28; 31; 35; 40; 52; 54; 55; 56; 59; 69; 70; 71; 104; 109; 139; 140; 141; 143

The refining of interpretation requires a look at the principal solutions that have been advanced regarding the imprecatory psalms in relation to Christian ethics. The legitimacy of these solutions must be evaluated. Also, these psalms must be located in their ancient Near Eastern context, in which "cursing" was an everyday facet of life. A detailed exploration of the three harshest psalms of imprecation (Pss. 58; 137; 109) should uncover theological foundations upon which their cries were uttered. The results of this investigation must be viewed through the apparent contradictory statements of certain New Testament texts. These include the command of Jesus to "love your enemies" and of Paul to "bless, and curse not." The backdrop of the imprecations in the Psalms, coupled with imprecations in the New Testament, can give deeper, fuller understanding of these statements.

It seems better to approach the issue at hand from a biblical-theological, rather than a systematic-theological, standpoint. Therefore, the progress and fullness of Scripture is investigated as the limits of ethical inquiry. In addressing, for example, concerns relating to the "rightness" of God's vengeance and violence against the wicked it is assumed that the Bible's own testimony—by assertion or example—accurately teaches what is right. For Christians who view the Bible as the Word of God,[35] it stands as the singular rule for "life and godliness" (2 Peter 1:3). This approach entails recognition of a direct connection between the testaments: all Scripture speaks alike of the same God[36] and essentially the same people of God,[37] governed by essentially the same ethic.[38]

Indeed, the New Testament, by its own testimony and inference, is both the necessary complement to and completion of the Old.[39]

Part 1

Contemporary Solutions
and Ancient Context

One

Unsatisfactory Solutions

Across the centuries, much has been written about the relationship of the Christian to cries of imprecation found in the Psalms. Yet even in modern treatments of this vital issue, there have been little more than cursory efforts to integrate imprecations holistically into the larger transtestamental biblical theology. As a result, the solutions proposed have proven theologically inadequate. Some of these solutions are

1. Imprecatory psalms express evil emotions that should be suppressed or confessed as sin.
2. They are utterances consonant with old covenant morality but inconsistent with new covenant ethics.
3. Such words may be appropriately spoken only by Christ in relation to his work on the cross and only by his followers through him.

Evil Emotions

Not to Be Expressed

The esteemed C. S. Lewis, whose works have been a wellspring of inspiration, finds that "in some of the Psalms the spirit of hatred which strikes us in the face is like the heat from a furnace mouth,"—and "perhaps the worst is in 109." But "even more devilish in one verse is the, otherwise beautiful, 137 where a blessing is pronounced on anyone who will snatch up a Babylonian baby and beat its brains out against the pavement."[1] Lewis uses such phrases to describe these psalms as "terrible or (dare we say?) contemptible,"[2] "wicked" and "sinful,"[3] "ferocious" and "dangerous."[4] He further believes with regard to them that "we must face both facts squarely. The hatred is there—festering, gloating, undisguised—and also we should be wicked if we in any way condoned or approved it, or (worse still) used it to justify similar passions in ourselves."[5]

To embrace this position, however, is questionable on several counts.

First, to contend that imprecatory psalms pulsate with malice and revenge—unfit in those trained in the school of Christ to "love your enemies"—runs counter to the distinguishing feature of David. This principal author of at least twenty-three of the thirty-two psalms in question is styled in Scripture as "a man after [God's] own heart" (1 Sam. 13:14; cf. 16:7).[6] It would seem inconsistent that his character would receive such unqualified endorsement if he were to exhibit in these psalms a heart that is fundamentally far from the character of Christ.[7]

Scripture is not reticent to note the passions and sins of David. He succumbed to the temptation for rage and revenge (e.g., 1 Sam. 25:21–22). He committed heinous crimes—including adultery, deception, and murder (2 Sam. 11). These failings did not, however, express his prevailing character, which was rather revealed in his repentance (cf. Ps. 51; 1 Sam. 25:32–34).[8]

Moreover, David was quick to exhibit a Christlike spirit toward enemies, in particular, King Saul.[9] Indeed, his imprecations in the psalms are against enemies who had repeatedly returned "evil for good" or who had taken part in gross—and frequently sustained—injustice. In Psalm 35:12–14, for example, David relates this core practice of love in action:

> [12]They repay me evil for good—
>   what bereavement to my soul!
> [13]Yet I, when they were sick, I clothed myself in sackcloth;
>   I humbled myself in fasting,
>   but my prayers returned unanswered.
> [14]As though for my friend or brother, I paced back and forth;
>   as though mourning for my mother, I bowed my head in grief.

A second problem with the view that the imprecatory expressions are evil is that the purposes governing them and the principal themes running through them are of the highest ethical plane. These purposes and themes carry

- a concern for the honor of God (e.g., Ps. 74:22, "Rise up, O God, and defend your cause; remember how fools mock you all day long!");
- a concern for the realization of justice amid rampant injustice (e.g., Ps. 58:11, "Then men will say . . . 'Surely there is a God who judges in the earth!'");
- a concern for the public recognition of the sovereignty of God (e.g., Ps. 59:13, "Then it will be known to the ends of the earth that God rules over Jacob");
- a hope that divine retribution will cause the enemies to seek Yahweh (e.g., Ps. 83:17, "Fill their faces with shame so that they may seek your name");
- an abhorrence of sin (e.g., Ps. 139:21, "Do I not hate those who hate you, O Yahweh?");
- a concern for the preservation of the righteous (e.g., Ps. 143:11–12, "For the sake of your name, O Yahweh, preserve my life! . . . And in your loving-kindness annihilate my enemies and destroy all my foes, for I am your servant").

A third problem with maintaining that the expressions in the imprecatory psalms are evil, exuding a spirit far distant from the Spirit of God, is that this view implies a denial that the Psalms are inspired.[10] By the testimony of both David and David's greater Son, the Psalms come under the purview of divine inspiration. David's own attestation in 2 Samuel 23:2 is that "the Spirit of Yahweh spoke through me." As noted above, this same David wrote a large portion of the imprecatory psalms. In Mark 12:36, Jesus stated that "David himself spoke by the Holy Spirit," using this clause to introduce a quotation from the Psalms. Perhaps most pertinent, Peter quotes from both Psalms 69 and 109—two of the most "notorious" imprecatory psalms—preceded by the statement that these Scriptures "had to be fulfilled which *the Holy Spirit spoke long ago through the mouth of David* concerning Judas" (Acts 1:16, 20; cf. Pss. 69:25; 109:8, emphasis added).

Lewis himself recognized that his own view demanded that he make a certain compromise in his acceptance of the divine inspiration of the Psalms. Since he believed that the imprecatory psalms were "so full of that passion to which Our Lord's teaching allows no quarter," he courted the middle territory "that all Holy Scripture is in some sense—though not all parts of it in the same sense—the word of God."[11]

A fourth problem with condemning the imprecatory texts is that this view is contrary to the nature of the Psalms as a book fashioned for the worship of Yahweh by his people. To explain the imprecatory psalms as outbursts of evil emotion, not to be emulated, may well account for the initial writing of the Psalms, but it does not adequately explain why these texts were incorporated into the canon—indeed, the book of worship for God's people. George Gunn is perceptive in observing that to regard the imprecatory psalms

> as wholly vindictive may be a sufficient explanation for the *writing* of them, because anyone in certain given circumstances of distress and provocation may have surrendered to this dark spirit. What we have to account for, however, is not the writing of them but their incorporation into the Psalter at the time when it was compiled, and in view of the purpose for which it was compiled. It is as nearly certain as can be that there was a higher reason for their inclusion in a collection that was intended solely for use in the worship of God.[12]

Indeed, these troubling curses and cries for vengeance appear with such frequency that they form an integral part of the canonical Psalter,[13] and this without any literary or theological indication of divine disapproval at the expression of such sentiments.[14] Nor was there felt any need for later copyists and compilers to expunge such material as unbefitting the Book of God. Gunn further muses that there must be some expression in these psalms that the compilers "regarded as seemly and necessary in the people's approach to God in worship; and they took the risk—a very large one—of the misunderstanding which would arise and has constantly arisen from the type of language in which that thought was clothed."[15] Readers of Scripture must grapple with this reality.

Indeed, these cries' prevalence in the book of worship lends credence to the opinion that they are to be embraced as the believer's justified appeal to divine justice, rather than utterances to be desperately avoided.

To Be Expressed and Relinquished

Walter Brueggemann understands the imprecatory psalms to be hateful cries for revenge, cries that Christians must move beyond. Yet this way beyond the psalms of vengeance "is a way *through* them and not *around* them."[16] He wrote that, rather than disowning them, Christians ought fully to embrace these harsh psalms as their own. These texts voice a common sentiment, for humans are vengeful creatures. "Our rage and indignation must be fully owned and fully expressed. Then (and *only* then) can our rage and indignation be yielded to the mercy of God."[17]

Rather than proposing to ban such rage from the worship of God and the life of faith, he nobly insists that this "rage is rightly carried even to the presence of Yahweh,"[18] to be relinquished there.[19]

Brueggemann's position is commendable. First, it seeks to maintain the rightful place of the imprecatory psalms in the life of the Christian and in Christian worship. Second, it brings all of life to God in prayer as petitioners bow before his lordship. In still viewing these imprecations as "evil," however, Brueggemann fails to reckon fully with the Old Testament foundations of imprecation as well as the presence of similar expression in the New Testament. Indeed, the larger trans-testamental testimony appears to exonerate and, in limited and appropriate circumstances, even commend the texts. These "curses" are based upon the covenant promises of God. It seems apparent, then, that it would not be inherently evil for his people to petition him—albeit passionately—to fulfill these promises.

This yearning for God's just vengeance on the inveterately wicked is far from evil. Jesus himself displayed rage at stubborn sin: "He looked around at them in anger, deeply grieved at their stubborn hearts" (Mark 3:5). "Snakes! Brood of vipers! How will you escape being condemned to Gehenna?!" (Matt. 23:33). In both cases Christ reacted against the hardened unbelief and opposition of religious leaders.

Now, neither Matthew 23:33 nor Mark 3:5 is imprecatory, but both bear an imprecatory sense and intensity that fit the cornerstones of what Brueggemann sees as evil. These two texts certainly convey a yearning for divine vengeance,[20] expressed through the emotion of rage. And if such characterizes the sinless Savior, then a righteous "rage" has been reclaimed.[21]

Old Covenant Morality

Inferior Morality

Approaching the issue from a dispensational and progressive-revelational standpoint, Roy Zuck seeks to alleviate the difficulty aroused by the imprecatory psalms. He claims that "the unfolding of revealed truth in the Word of God is accompanied by a similar advancement of morals"[22] and that "the Old Testament is on a lower moral plane than the New Testament."[23] Of principal support for his thesis is the observation that, "though there are many passages which speak of tenderness and kindness toward others, even toward enemies, the Old Testament never speaks of *forgiving or loving avowed enemies of God.*"[24] This assertion is placed opposite the words of Christ urging his disciples to "love your enemies" (Matt. 5:44).

Zuck finds two passages in the Old Testament that speak of consideration for one's enemy—but that *consideration* does not, in his view, equal *love*. Exodus 23:4–5 rules as part of the law, "If you happen upon the stray ox or donkey of your enemy, you must surely return it to him. If you see the donkey of one who hates you fallen under its load, do not fail to help him; you must surely help him with it."

Proverbs 25:21 adds the ethical injunction, "If one who hates you is hungry, give him food to eat; if he is thirsty, give him water to drink."

To this perspective that the Old Testament lacks a concept of enemy-love, two principal objections can be offered. First, the narrow understanding of love placed upon the Old Testament (or the New, for that matter) is countered by the broader teaching and example of Scripture. In both testaments, love is expressed tangibly in acts of kindness, so a deed of kindness is viewed as an act of love.

Leviticus 19, for example, from which the "second great command-ment" arises, is replete with various "actions" that reveal a heart of love for one's neighbor—whether a native or an "outsider." These actions include such things as intentionally leaving the edges of the harvest field for the poor and the foreigner (vv. 9–10); paying your workers in a timely fashion (v. 13); showing respect for the elderly (v. 32); and treating the foreigner as if he were a native (v. 34). Indeed, in this latter passage, Yahweh goes on to command the Israelites to "love him [the foreigner] as yourself, for you were foreigners [גֵּרִים] in the land of Egypt."[25] This last passage helps us to understand that the reference to "loving your neighbor" in Leviticus 19:18, although parallel to "one of your people," is by no means meant to be confined there. Rather, that dictum is intended to apply to anyone nearby whose need you are able to meet, to whom you can show tangible love.

Such a dictate, in many ways, laid the foundation for Jesus' parable of the Good Samaritan in answer to the query, "Who is my neighbor?" (Luke 10:29–37).

Furthermore, in Matthew 5:45 (cf. Luke 6:35), Jesus established the command for *loving* one's enemies upon the example of the *kindness* of God, who "sends rain on the righteous and the unrighteous" alike. And this kindness toward one's enemies is without question both commanded (Exod. 23:4–5; Prov. 25:21) and modeled in the Old Testament (e.g., Naaman's slave girl in 2 Kings 5;[26] Elisha in 2 Kings 6:15–23;[27] and Jonah's reluctant witness to Nineveh in Jonah 3–4[28]).

To distance deeds of kindness from the definition of love would be to limit without warrant the intent of Scripture. Thus, the Old Testament does indeed speak of loving one's enemies—but this enemy-love is placed in the language, command, and example of enemy-kindness, *which is love in action.*

Second, the attempts to explain the ethics of the imprecatory psalms as inferior to ethics of the new covenant runs counter to a proper under-standing of progressive revelation. F. G. Hibbard offers an insightful explanation for the nature of progressive revelation: God withholding from one age what he has bestowed upon a subsequent one. "But what the Holy Spirit actually commanded, or inspired the Old Testament writers to utter, on moral subjects, is, and must be, in harmony with absolute morality."[29] There is indeed a degree of difference in the progress of the testaments; but it is a difference in degree not in kind. For *"in essence there is only one principle in regard to morals pervading the Scriptures."*[30]

This essential moral principle is articulated by Jesus, who asserted that the two "great commands" given in the Old Testament are the same two "great commands" reinforced in the New. When he was tested by one of the Pharisees with the question, "Teacher, what is the greatest commandment in the Law?" Jesus replied, "'Love the Lord your God with all your heart and with all your soul and with all your mind.' This is the greatest and first commandment. And the second is like it: 'Love your neighbor as yourself.' On these two commandments hang all the Law and the Prophets" (Matt. 22:36–40). From Jesus' own testimony, then, the morality of the new covenant in its highest expression is constant with that of the Old Testament.[31]

The way that morality is expressed within the varying dispensations, however, may indeed vary. This is due, among other things, to the centralized status of God's people in the Old Testament versus their decentralized status in the New. In the Old Testament, God's people were surrounded by enemy nations: the necessity of their survival and the fulfillment of God's promises required a prevailing posture of caution or defense.[32] But with the coming of Christ and the outpouring of the Spirit as the culmination of the ages and the climax of promise has come a more explicit embrace of enemy-love and enduring abuse[33] and the opening of the nations to the gospel of grace.

Chalmers Martin distances the Christian from imprecatory prayers when he asserts that the "distinction between the sin and the sinner was impossible to David as an Old Testament saint."[34] He adds that this distinction must now be made. According to Martin, the progress of revelation alters the Christian's stance toward the enemies of God from one of enmity against the whole being to one of mere hatred of the governing principle of sin operating through the sinner.[35]

However common this sentiment may implicitly be in modern Christendom,[36] it insufficiently characterizes the broader theology of Scripture. The position of Scripture is not only "Love the sinner but hate the sin," but also paradoxically "Love the sinner but hate the sinner." Even in the New Testament, the fullness of revelation's progress, it is *sinners—*

not just sin—who will be destroyed, suffering the eternal torment of hell.[37] McKenzie rightly observes that "sin as an abstraction has no existence. The sin which we hate has its concrete existence in human wills."[38] He then perceptively muses,

> There is a lawful hatred of the sinner; and indeed there must be, since such a hatred is the obverse of the love of God. The love of God hates all that is opposed to God; and sinners—not merely sin—are opposed to God. And if such a sentiment is lawful, its expression is lawful; and one may desire that the evil in another receive its corresponding evil—provided that this hatred is restrained within the limits of that which is lawful. These limits are: 1. Hatred must not be directed at the *person* of one's neighbor; he is hated *for his evil quality.* 2. One may desire that the divine justice be accomplished in the sinner; but it must be a desire for divine justice, not a desire for the personal evil of another out of personal revenge. 3. The infliction of evil may not be desired absolutely, but only under the condition that the sinner remains obdurate and unrepentant. 4. It must be accompanied by that true supernatural charity which efficaciously desires the supreme good—the eternal happiness—of all men in general, not excluding any individual who is capable of attaining it. In a word, the sinner may lawfully be hated only when he is loved.[39]

On the part of God, this seeming paradox of "loving yet hating the sinner" is exhibited as God rains both judgment and blessing upon the unrighteous. It is seen in the comparison of Psalm 11:5–6 ("the wicked and him who loves violence his soul hates. He will rain on the wicked coals of fire[40] and sulfur") to Matthew 5:44–45 ("Love your enemies . . . so that you may be sons of your Father who is in heaven; for he . . . sends rain on the righteous and the unrighteous"). Isaiah 63:3–4 ("I trampled them in my anger . . . their blood splattered my garments . . . for the day of vengeance was in my heart") can be compared with Ezekiel 33:11("I take no pleasure in the death of the wicked, but that the wicked turn from his way and live"). As John Piper ponders upon this paradox, he observes that "God is grieved in one sense by the death of the wicked, and pleased in another." This is evidence of what he labels "the infinitely complex emotional life of God."[41] God is able simultaneously to both love and hate unbelievers—loving them in the sense that he lavishly distributes his common grace, and hating them in the sense that they stand as rebellious sinners before a holy God.

And this life of God is a life the Christian is to emulate—albeit in a vastly inferior manner.[42] As far as the finite Christian is able to reflect the character and sentiment of God, he or she is called to do so.[43] The pattern for this endeavor is Christ, who lived pervasive love yet did not shy away from denouncing the unrepentant wicked—even the "religious" one.[44] On the Christian's part, then, this tension is lived out practically and particularly with regard to hardened sinners deemed "beyond the ken of repentance."[45] Imprecations of judgment against them are uttered *"on the hypothesis of their continued impenitence."*[46] Under such circumstances, "to wipe out the sins results in the destruction of the sinner."[47] This is most often seen in the necessity of public justice executed against flagrant criminals. And it is against men such as these—"bloodthirsty men"—that David cried, "Do I not hate those who hate you, O Yahweh?" (Ps. 139:21).[48]

Differing Dispensations

In a distinct but related dispensational approach, J. Carl Laney sees the issue as one, not of progress in ethics, but simply of differing dispensations. He astutely observes that "the fundamental ground on which one may justify the imprecations in the Psalms is the covenantal basis for the curse on Israel's enemies"[49] as found in the Abrahamic covenant of Genesis 12:1–3, which promised blessing on those who blessed Abraham's seed and cursing on those who cursed them. But because he views Abraham's seed as including solely those of the race and nation of Israel, he asserts that "it would be inappropriate for a church-age believer to call down God's judgment on the wicked."[50]

This position, however, ignores the manifest presence of imprecations on the lips of saints in the "dispensation of grace." Also, it runs counter to the testimony of the New Testament, which affirms the enduring validity of the Abrahamic promise for those who embrace Christ through faith (cf. Gal. 3:6–29).[51] Laney's restriction of the Abrahamic promise to "Israel according to the flesh" (1 Cor. 10:18) is parried by Paul's proclamation in Galatians 3:29 (cf. Rom. 2:28–29) that "if you belong to Christ, then you belong to Abraham's seed, [and are thus] heirs according to the promise." And if one is an heir of the Abrahamic covenant through Christ, one is an heir—in some fundamental measure at least—to its related promises of blessing and cursing found therein.[52]

Although Meredith Kline approaches the problem from a covenantal perspective, he comes to a conclusion similar to the dispensational positions. He posits that the old covenant witnesses to "intrusion ethics," so the ethics of the consummation have been "intruded" into the era of common grace. He believes that the ethics of the Sinaitic covenant in particular are "an anticipatory abrogation of the principle of common grace"[53] inappropriate for the New Testament age, but which will be realized as the ethics of the age to come. At that time, believers "will have to change their attitude toward the unbeliever from one of neighborly love to one of perfect hatred."[54] The imprecatory psalms, then, in their expressions of hatred and their cries for vengeance, belong to this divine abrogation of common grace and, as such, could not be legitimately echoed by the Christian church.

One of the principles of common grace, Kline asserts, is that "we may not seek to destroy those for whom, perchance, Christ has died."[55] Harry Mennega shares Kline's sentiment, claiming that

> we do not by special revelation know who are and who are not reprobate, as the psalmists of old did. We can therefore never use these psalms to refer them to particular individuals or groups of individuals who at any specific time by their actions display enmity at God's kingdom. Those who are enemies of God at present may be his choice vessels tomorrow.[56]

However true this latter statement may be, to the larger construction it must be objected that nowhere in Scripture is it affirmed that the psalmists knew by God's Spirit who, in the divine decree, were reprobate.[57] They did know, however, who were the inveterate enemies of God and his people. Neither does Scripture categorically forbid the cry for judgment against such people. Zuck rightly admits the presence of unmistakable imprecations in the present era. He cites 1 Corinthians 16:22; Galatians 1:8–9; 5:12; 2 Timothy 4:14; and Revelation 6:9–10. He explains these imprecations by saying that they are voiced against "those who are the avowed adversaries of the Lord" and "who are inexorably opposed and relentlessly antagonistic to the gospel of Jesus Christ."[58] Zuck's point, it ought to be noted, is the very point of the Old Testament imprecations. They also are voiced against the hardened adversaries of God.

Christians are never called to make the unerring judgment delineating those who are "permanently identified with the kingdom of evil."[59] But Christ himself has given the guiding principle by which to detect, in a practical manner,[60] the elect from the reprobate: "By their fruit you shall know them" (Matt. 7:16, 20).[61]

H. G. L. Peels also believes that, although it is incorrect to condemn the Old Testament imprecatory prayer from the perspective of New Testament ethics, "it is also impossible within the New Testament situation to raise the imprecatory prayer in the same manner as was done by the psalmists of the Old Testament."[62] He bases this perspective on the fundamental change that has occurred in the Cross. Indeed, the imprecatory prayer "must necessarily undergo modification because the cross of Christ is the definitive, visible revelation of God's justice."[63] He argues that the imprecatory prayer, when properly transformed into a New Testament context, would be characterized by an eschatological and partially spiritualized focus. It "could take the form of a general anathema against all opposing powers"[64]—especially the kingdom and power of the Evil One.

Two objections to the position of Peels, however, can be noted. First, while indeed more explicit emphasis is placed on the spiritual warfare of New Testament saints and their eschatological hope, as expanded and clarified in the progress of revelation, both elements were central in the experience of Old Testament saints as well. They had daily awareness of the opposing "gods" of the various surrounding nations,[65] and they looked in hope to the age to come in its varied facets, as was repeatedly stated by the prophets.[66]

The second objection regards the presence of extreme, personal curses in the New Testament, with no implication of condemnation attached to them. Of particular note are Acts 8:20 and Galatians 1:9. Peter cursed Simon the Sorcerer when he sought to purchase the power of the Holy Spirit: "To hell with you and your money!"[67] (Acts 8:20). Paul issued a vehement "anathema" against the Judaizers who had infiltrated the Galatian churches and proclaimed a "gospel" of legalism: "If anyone preaches a gospel to you other than the one you received, let him be damned!" (Gal. 1:9). These curses draw a definite conclusion about the opponents' eternal status in the decree of God, while implying or offering hope of repentance (e.g., Acts 8:22).

Although the justice of God *was* definitively revealed in the cross of Christ, such revelation does not relieve the persistent injustices against God's people nor wholly assuage their justification for calling down God's justice (e.g., Luke 18:1–8). Nor do the words of Christ from the cross, "Father, forgive them" (Luke 23:34),[68] mute their plea. Rather, the New Testament continues to record petitions for divine vengeance on the lips of earth-bound and heaven-arrived saints alike (notably Rev. 6:9–10).[69]

Songs of Christ

The question is sometimes asked, "Who is the 'I' of the Psalms? Who is it that petitions the destruction of enemies?" Is it the individual believer or the covenant community? Is it David or the Davidic monarch? Or is it Christ himself who prays these prayers, and the Christian through him? Indeed, for James Adams, this "is really the critical issue with the imprecatory psalms. If *you* were to ask God to destroy your personal enemy, that would be in essence cursing that enemy and, therefore, sinful. But if the King of Peace asks God to destroy *His* enemies, that is another matter!"[70] Adams further states that these psalms are not "the emotional prayers of angry men, but the very war cries of our Prince of Peace!"[71] Indeed, these psalms "can only be grasped when heard from the loving lips of our Lord Jesus."[72]

In this Adams concurs with Dietrich Bonhoeffer, the German martyr of World War II, who argues that, although David did, in fact, utter these prayers of imprecation against his enemies, he did so only as the "prototype of Jesus Christ,"[73] who was to arise from David's line. "Or better," he refines, "Christ himself prayed them through his forerunner David."[74] It is only out of this relationship and understanding that the individual Christian may echo, "insofar as he participates in Christ and his community and prays their prayer."[75]

Bonhoeffer views the imprecatory psalms as prayers, not so much for the execution of God's vengeance on instances of gross injustice, as for the execution of God's judgment on sin in general—a judgment in history that is fully and solely satisfied in the cross of Christ:

> God's vengeance did not strike the sinners, but the one sinless man who stood in the sinners' place, namely God's own Son. Jesus Christ bore the wrath of God, for the execution of which the psalm prays. He stilled God's wrath toward sin and prayed in the hour of the execution of the divine judgment: 'Father, forgive them, for they do not know what they do!' . . . God hates and redirects his enemies to the only righteous one, and this one asks forgiveness for them. . . . Thus the imprecatory psalm leads to the cross of Jesus and to the love of God which forgives enemies. I cannot forgive the enemies of God out of my own resources. Only the crucified Christ can do that, and I through Him. . . . In this way the crucified Jesus teaches us to pray the imprecatory psalms correctly.[76]

Divine justice toward the redeemed *was* fully satisfied in the Cross; however, divine justice toward the reprobate cannot be fully satisfied, except in the torments of eternal hell.[77] And it is out of the scourges of injustice from such reprobates that the cry of the righteous arises. In addition, while David does, indeed, function as a forerunner of Christ, his words were spoken out of his emotions as a person who lived in the midst of history. Deferring all the significance of these Davidic psalms of imprecation until the cross of Christ distances them from their historical setting and robs them of their power as archetypes.[78]

Adams's and Bonhoeffer's proposed solutions also do not adequately answer the problem that imprecations were included in psalms that David, the type of Christ, did not write. Not all of the imprecatory psalms designate David as their author (notably Ps. 137),[79] an objection that is not satisfactorily addressed by subsuming all of the Psalms under the aegis of his name.[80] Nor does David as forerunner speak the cries for divine vengeance in other parts of Scripture. If imprecations against one's enemies and the enemies of God are deemed morally appropriate in other parts of Scripture, and these are not rendered legitimate by placing them on the lips of Christ, then this proposal offers no solution to the issues of imprecation in the Psalms or of imprecation in general.

Numerous proposed solutions have been offered to relate imprecatory psalms to Christian ethics. Although these solutions address the issue from vastly differing perspectives, it is significant that each explanation ends up distancing the imprecatory psalms from legitimate prayers of God's people today.[81] This distance is fundamentally foreign to the use of the psalms as they were passed down through history. Indeed, the Psalter in its entirety was incorporated into the Christian canon with the tacit affirmation that it remained a book of worship for God's people.[82]

If it was appropriate for an Old Testament saint to utter such prayers against the vicious enemies of God and his people, then it is appropriate for us to do so as well.[83] In embracing the tensions inherent in this understanding, the Christian must maintain a peculiar balance. As Martin Luther expressed it, "We should pray that our enemies be converted and become our friends and, if not, that their doing and designing be bound to fail and have no success and that their persons perish rather than the Gospel and the kingdom of Christ."[84]

Two

Curse in Its Cultural Context

The use of "the curse" in the Psalms and elsewhere in Scripture shocks modern Western sensibilities. But these imprecations arise out of a cultural milieu in which cursing was an integral part of life[1]—both domestic and international, personal and covenantal. For evidence, consider the numerous examples of treaty curses, inscriptional curses, and incantations to undo curses that have been found. Indeed, the psalmists of Israel drew on a common ancient Near Eastern curse tradition:

> The curse played a significant role in the daily life of the ancient Middle East. In all areas of private as well as communal life (social-economic, juridical, cultic, political) the practice of cursing was applied. The curse was to bring the truth to light (in juridical procedures, e.g., in the ordeal), force obedience (with treaties and regulations), frighten off thieves, plunderers and vandals (with inscriptions on graves, boundary stones and buildings), guarantee honesty (in economic transactions), etc. The oath, which was uttered under a vast number of circumstances, is a form of self-cursing. The deity could also employ the curse as a preventive measure or in punishment.[2]

The mere presence of the kinds of curses and calls for divine vengeance found in the Psalms would not have aroused the moral indignation of an ancient Israelite. These would not have been regarded as shocking or hate-

36

ful outbursts. Rather, a "legitimate" curse was distinguished from an "illegitimate" curse. One was proper and the other reprehensible. The illegitimate curse was uttered out of malice against an innocent party to effect personal gain, or "as a private means of revenge to smite a personal enemy,"[3] often in secret and with the aid of magic. The legitimate curse was uttered to cover egregious infractions of the moral order, often in a public forum with appeal to deity. Notably, it is this legitimate kind of curse that we find uttered in the imprecatory psalms.

Moreover, in the Psalms,

> it is precisely the godless enemy to whom such illegitimate curses are attributed. . . . The psalmist, with his imprecatory prayer, does not commit the same sin as his enemies. His prayer, including the curse formulations, is fundamentally of another nature and posits justice against injustice, the appeal of God in contrast to the cursing of the godless.[4]

Furthermore, in the community of Israel, as in the broader ancient Near East, the legitimate curse was an expression of human powerlessness. It was used when people were unable to adequately help or protect themselves. This cry was the voice of the oppressed, the victim, and the unjustly accused. It was directed against powerful or unconvictable offenders.[5] Indeed, the legitimate curse was an act of faith that God's desire for justice, as expressed in the Law and ethical teachings of religion, would be reflected in real life. When viewed in this light, the so-called imprecatory psalms and other imprecatory texts, which seem so vicious and strange to the modern reader, are seen to be expressions of faith in the just rule of Yahweh in situations in which the covenant member or community can see no other source of help or possible means of securing just treatment.[6]

The Function of Imprecation in the Ancient Near East

Treaty Curses

Ancient Near Eastern suzerain-vassal treaties, as a genre, generally conform to a consistent pattern of basic elements:

- The *preamble* introduces the setting and the suzerain, extolling him in grandiose terms.
- The *historical prologue* delineates the past relationship between the two parties.
- The *stipulations*, the nucleus of the covenant, state the obligations imposed upon, and accepted by, the vassal.
- *Arrangements* are stated for storage and transmission of the treaty document.
- The *list of witnesses* principally calls on divinities, who are invoked to exact punishment should the covenant be broken.
- The *blessings and curses* of the covenant relationship are specified—blessings for obedience to the covenant and curses for disobedience.

The purpose of these promised blessings and curses was to ensure the vassal's loyalty to the sovereign and to the covenant. Although the suzerain played an active role in bestowing favor and taking retribution in relation to the vassal, the blessings and curses were not to be fulfilled primarily by him. Rather, this section specified what the *gods* would do if the treaty provisions were faithfully kept or if they were violated.[7] This understanding lays the groundwork in the mind of the faithful Israelite that the fulfillment of the curse must be left up to God.

It is out of this understanding that the imprecatory psalm is uttered.

Covenant curses of the ancient Near East are pronounced upon the totality of the vassal's life and the lives of everyone in his family. The Hittite treaty between Mursilis and Duppi-Tessub of Amurru concisely demonstrates the reach of such curses: "Should Duppi-Tessub not honor these words of the treaty and the oath, may these gods of the oath destroy Duppi-Tessub together with his person, his wife, his son, his grandson, his house, his land and together with everything that he owns."[8] These curses, here stated in Hittite brevity, are expanded in exhaustive and often hideous detail in the Assyrian vassal treaties of Esarhaddon, parallels of which may be found in Deuteronomy 28.[9] The distilled essence of the pronounced curses, however, is the request that Ashur, king of the gods, "[decree for you] evil and not good."[10] The following excerpts from the extensive curses of this Assyrian treaty flesh out what the preceding synopsis entails:

May he never grant you fatherhood and attainment of old age.[11]
....
[May Sin], the brightness of heaven and earth, clothe you with
[a lep]rosy; [may he forbid your entering into the presence of the
    gods]
[or king (saying): "Roam the desert] like the wild-ass (and) the
    gazelle."
[May Shamash, the light of the heavens and] earth [not]
[judge] you justly (saying): "May it be dark
in your eyes, walk in darkness."[12]
[May Ninurta, chief of the gods,] fell you with his swift arrow;
[may he fill] the plain [with your corpses;] may he feed
your flesh to the eagle (and) jackal.
[May Venus, the brightest of the stars,] make your wives
lie [in the lap of your enemy before your eyes]; may your sons
[not possess your house]; may a foreign enemy divide your goods.[13]
....
May they make your ground (hard) like iron so that
[none] of you may f[lourish].
Just as rain does not fall from a brazen heaven[14]
so may rain and dew not come upon your fields
and your meadows; may it rain burning
coals instead of dew on your land.[15]
....
Just as a starving ewe puts
[the flesh of her young] in her mouth, even so
may he feed you in your hunger
with the flesh of your brothers, your sons (and) your daughters.[16]
....
[As oil en]ters your flesh,
[just so may] they cause this curse to enter
into your flesh,[17] [the flesh of your brothers],
your sons and your daughters.[18]

The Syrian treaty between a certain Bir-Gaʾyah and Matiʿel of Arpad
witnesses to a profuse display of ritually underscored curses against the

person of Matiᶜel and his nobles should they betray their loyalty, and curses against any who would mar or fail to guard the inscribed treaty. After introducing the gods of the two nations as witnesses, the treaty lists "futility" curses on the land and its fertility.

It is significant to note that the fulfillment of these curses is under the purview of the witnessing gods: "[May Ha]dad [pour (over it)] every sort of evil (which exists) on earth and in heaven and every sort of trouble; and may he shower upon Arpad [ha]il-[stones]! . . . May the gods send every sort of devourer against Arpad and against its people!"[19] Following this, word is united with vivid ritual, to reinforce and dramatize the curse: "Just as this wax is burned by fire, so shall Matî[ᶜel be burned by fi]re. . . . [Just as] this calf is cut in two, so may Matîᶜel be cut in two and may his nobles be cut in two."[20]

And the treaty concludes with a curse, under divine enforcement, on any who would even deface the treaty inscription: "Whoever will not guard the words of the inscription which is on this stele or will say, 'I shall efface some of his (its) words' . . . on any day on which he will do so, may the gods overturn th[at m]an and his house and all that (is) in it."[21]

As the ancient Near Eastern treaty called down curses upon the vassal who breaks covenant with his suzerain, so also did many of the imprecatory psalms. The curses found therein are frequently voiced because the psalmist views his enemy as having grossly violated the covenant. As a consequence, the covenant breaker deserves the covenant curses. Thus, the psalmist cries out to the God of the covenant. And as the treaty curses were viewed as extending not only to the offender but also to his children, so also the curses in the Psalms are seen to extend at times to the enemy's posterity (notably Pss. 109:9–13; 137:8–9).

Inscriptional Curses

In addition to their role in ancient Near Eastern treaties, curses—without accompanying blessings—are characteristically found in inscriptions on tombs, statues, and boundary stones (*kudurrus*).[22]

These inscriptional curses warn of dire consequences against any who would change, move, deface, or rob the monument to which they are attached. They "appear to be the last resort in situations when conventional means fail to provide needed security: where hidden tombs cannot defeat the cleverness of grave robbers, where respect for the dead does not prevent the living from jealously effacing a predecessor's name from a record of his or her accomplishments,"[23] or where the promise of economic gain overshadows common respect for another's property. Thus, as with the imprecatory psalms, inscriptional curses were uttered out of a context of powerlessness, and their fulfillment was placed with the deity. The gods are explicitly[24] or implicitly[25] called to enforce the curse should the threats be ignored; the curses do not of themselves "magically" come into force.

Incantations to Undo Curses

The legitimate curse in ancient Mesopotamia, which sought to protect from harm or to pray for justice, "was a highly developed legal and religious ceremony, universally practiced and respected. It not only figured in ceremonies of great occasions, but also penetrated into the everyday life of the people."[26] The prevalence of curses is shown by the numerous records of Assyrian incantation rituals to undo curses. The three principal collections are *Maqlû, Šurpu,* and *Utukki Limnûti.* By means of these rites, the sufferer seeks release from the effects of a curse placed by a malevolent witch, demon, or unknown cause.

In the series *Maqlû* (burning), "the longest and most important Mesopotamian text concerned with combating witchcraft,"[27] a curse "is pronounced upon those who have bewitched the complainant and thus caused him to suffer."[28] The ritual begins with a description of the supplicant's status of suffering brought about by the supposed witch's curse:

> I have called upon you Gods of the Night:
> . . . .
> Because a witch has bewitched me,
> A deceitful woman has accused me,
> Has (thereby) caused my god and goddess to be estranged
>   from me (and)
> I have become sickening in the sight of those who behold me,
> I am therefore unable to rest day or night,

> . . . .
> Because evil did she perform against me, and baseless charges
>   has she conjured up against me,
> May she die, but I live![29]

The climax of this complex ceremony is the declarative wish to reverse the original curse:[30] "The witch who bewitched me, with the witchcraft with which she bewitched me, bewitch her!"[31] Voiced again, "May
the curse of my mouth extinguish the curse of your mouth!"[32] And, as its
name "burning" implies, wax or wooden figurines of the sorcerer or—
more often—the sorceress who bewitched the supplicant are melted or
burnt in the fire, and the conjurations that compose this series address,
with very few exceptions, either these witches—in effigy—or the fire-
god who is to destroy them.[33]

The series *Šurpu,* although it also means "burning," is a rite of personal purification from an unknown offense rather than the retributive
sympathetic magic of *Maqlû.* In this ceremony, the sufferer seeks release
from the ill effects of some presumable sin of omission or commission,
by which he has "offended the gods and the existing world-order."[34]

> An evil curse like a *gallû*-demon has come upon (this) man,
> dumbness (and) daze have come upon him,
> an unwholesome dumbness has come upon him,
> evil curse, oath, headache.
> An evil curse has slaughtered this man like a sheep,
> his god left his body,
> his goddess . . . usually full of concern for him, has stepped aside.
> Dumbness (and) daze have covered him like a cloak and over-
>   whelm him incessantly.
> . . . .
> "Go, my son Marduk!
> Take him to the pure house of ablutions,
> undo his oath, release his oath,
> that the disturbing evil of his body,
> —be it the curse of his father,
> be it the curse of his mother,

> be it the curse of his elder brother,
> be it the curse of a bloodshed unknown to him—
> by pronouncing the charm of Ea the oath
> may be peeled off like (this) onion,
> stripped off like (these) dates,
> unraveled like (this) matting.
> Oath, be adjured by the name of heaven, be adjured by the name
>   of the earth!"[35]

In *Utukki Limnûti,* "Evil Spirits," the third major collection of Mesopotamian magical incantations, the afflicted pleads for deliverance from the curse of bodily illness, believed to have been caused by demonic influence:

> The evil Demon that like a cloak enshroudeth the man,
> The evil Ghost, the evil Devil that seize upon the body,
> The Hag-demon (and) Ghoul that smite the body with sickness,
> . . . .
> An evil curse hath settled on his body,
> Evil (and) sin on his body they have cast,
> Venom (and) wickedness have settled on him,
> Evil they have cast (upon him).
> The evil man, he whose face is evil, he whose mouth is evil, he
>   whose tongue is evil,
> Evil spell, witchcraft, sorcery,
> Enchantment, and all evil,
> Which rest on the body of the sick man.[36]

Notice even here, in an incantation ostensibly directed against demons, that the human element of cursing through word and magic is connected.

The Power of the Curse

It has been commonly alleged that, in the practice of the larger ancient Near Eastern world, the curse was viewed as "*automatic or self-fulfilling,* having the nature of a 'spell,' the very words of which were thought to possess reality and the power to effect the desired results."[37] In this view, according to ancient opinion, the power of the curse was inherent in its form, and the more powerful the speaker, the more powerful the curse. A certain measure of support for this view has been legitimately derived from the Mesopotamian incantation series, in which, even though there is periodic appeal to deity to effect the curse's release, the essence of the incantations is magical. Established word and rite effect the desired release. Reflecting upon this intimate connection between fervent prayer and symbolic act, Josef Scharbert expresses the prevalent impression "that people in the ancient Near East actually believed that the gods could be forced by such formulas and acts to intervene in the manner desired."[38]

Whereas, however, a measure of evidence can be presented that the broader ancient Near Eastern world embraced to some extent a magical view of the power of the curse—particularly with regard to the curses of witches and the incantations to undo these curses—this view was by no means embraced wholesale. Rather, it was a fundamental belief that the gods were the ones under whose jurisdiction lay the execution of at least the formal legitimate curses. This belief is shown by a number of extant treaty and inscriptional curses. In these treaties and inscriptions, it is either explicitly stated that the gods will enact the curses, or that thought is strongly implied. Nothing in these texts hints that inherent virtue resides in the words themselves. The power of the curse lay in the authority of the gods.

Against this reasoning, it is argued that the passive voice is used predominantly in Hebrew curse formulas (אָרוּר, ʾārûr, i.e., "cursed be"). One theory is that the passive is used because there is an inherent power in the words; no divine agency is needed to fulfill them. But this supposition overlooks the larger testimony of the Old Testament, in which Yahweh himself is either the implicit or explicit agent behind the curse. Indeed, in the theology of orthodox Israel, nothing operates independently of God. He is the ground of all being and the source of all power—including the power of blessing and cursing. Apart from his will, no curse is effected.[39] In his sovereignty he can transmute cursing into blessing[40] and blessing into cursing.[41] Notably, in the inaugural promise to Abraham, which forms the basis upon which Yahweh's covenant with his people throughout the Scriptures is built, the active voice of the verb is used, and Yahweh is the explicit actor (אָאֹר, *ʾāʾôr*). Therein, Yahweh emphatically places upon himself the prerogative for the enforcement of curses uttered against his people. In Genesis 12:3, Yahweh declares, "He who curses you *I will curse*." And it is this declaration that forms the foundation for all personal curses uttered out of the covenant context.

Thus, in the life of Israel, and for the heirs of her religion, the effect of the spoken curse depends wholly on the will of Yahweh. Herbert Brichto remarks that the religion of Israel stands in stark contrast to the ideology of her surroundings. Mesopotamia is steeped in magic, but Israel is unrelenting in its campaign against it. In Mesopotamia, even the gods are subject to the forces of magic. In Israel, Yahweh is supremely independent of outside power; indeed, he is the source of all power.[42]

Moreover (as will be seen below), the Hebrew curse is either a veiled or blatant appeal to this God of justice to exact the punishment due for the guilt of the one cursed. For this cause, the Hebrew proverb can confidently assert, "Like a fluttering sparrow, like a darting swallow, so an undeserved curse does not come to rest" (Prov. 26:2). Thus, in contrast to the broader concept of the curse in the ancient Near East—which allowed the curious blend of both divine and automatic enactment—the curse in Israel entirely loses its magical character.[43] What remains is a sovereign, just, and compassionate covenant God.

Part 2

The Three Harshest Psalms

Three

Blood Bath: Psalm 58

Curse Against a Societal Enemy

For the director of music: "Do Not Destroy"; a *miktam* of David.

[1]Do you indeed, O "gods,"[1] decree what is right?
    Do you judge with equity, O sons of men?
[2]No, in your heart you plan injustice;
    in the earth you weigh out the violence of your hands.
[3]The wicked are estranged from the womb;
    they go astray from birth, speaking lies.
[4]Their venom is like the venom of a serpent,
    like a deaf cobra that stops its ears,
[5]that does not heed the sound of the charmers,
    the skillful binders of spells.
[6]O God, smash their teeth in their mouths;
    Break off the fangs of the young lions, O Yahweh!
[7]Let them flow away like water that runs off in all directions;
    let him prepare to shoot his arrows, only to find them headless![2]
[8]Like a miscarriage,[3] let him melt away;
    like a woman's abortion, let them not see the sun!
[9]Before your pots perceive (the heat of) the brambles—
    as "alive" as wrath—may he sweep them away!

[10]The righteous will rejoice when he sees vengeance;
    he will bathe his feet in the blood of the wicked.
[11]Then men will say, "Surely there is a reward for the righteous;
    surely there is a God who judges in the earth!"

—Psalm 58

Intended Recipients

When considering the imprecatory nature of this individual lament, two questions must be answered: (1) Who are being cursed? (2) What kind of people are they? The objects of David's imprecations are the rulers or "judges" of the community—those whose position involves ensuring that justice is properly meted out. Indeed, Psalm 58 is framed by an ironic inclusion of judicial ideas: The human "you judge" (v. 1) contrasts with the divine "who judges" (v. 11). The human "gods" (v. 1) contrasts with the divine "God" (v. 11). The lack of human justice "in the earth" (v. 2) is answered by the hope of divine justice "in the earth" (v. 11). The human perversion of "righteousness" (v. 1) provokes the divine vindication of the "righteous" (v. 11).

The identity of these "gods" as the leaders of the land is borne out by the context of this psalm and by its sibling, Psalm 82. In Psalm 82, the rulers of the people are spoken of as "gods." In structure, development of theme, and manner of address, Psalm 82 is much like Psalm 58. Although Psalm 82 begins with the imagery of the divine assembly over which God presides, it condescends immediately to the realm intended by that imagery—corrupt human leadership. Even these "gods" will yet die like men (v. 7).[4] In 58:1, the psalmist enlists sarcasm to address these "gods of government"[5] to inquire if they are exercising their authority according to the standards of God's supreme authority.

The character of these individuals is described as unjust (vv. 1–2), chronically dishonest (v. 3), ferociously violent (vv. 2, 6), stubbornly wicked and deadly (vv. 3–5), yet these individuals serve in a societal capacity, where justice should pervade. F. G. Hibbard notes an enlightening illustration in this regard, which once occurred during family worship:

I happened to be reading one of the imprecatory psalms, and as I paused to remark, my little boy, a lad of ten years, asked with some earnestness: "Father, do you think it right for a good man to pray for the destruction of his enemies like that?" and at the same time referred me to Christ as praying for his enemies. I paused a moment to know how to shape the reply so as to fully meet and satisfy his enquiry, and then said, "My son, if an assassin should enter the house by night, and murder your mother, and then escape, and the sheriff and citizens were all out in pursuit, trying to catch him, would you not pray to God that they might succeed and arrest him, and that he might be brought to justice?" "Oh, yes!" said he, "but I never saw it so before. I did not know that that was the meaning of these Psalms." "Yes," said I, "my son, the men against whom David prays were bloody men, men of falsehood and crime, enemies to the peace of society, seeking his own life, and unless they were arrested and their wicked devices defeated, many innocent persons must suffer." The explanation perfectly satisfied his mind.[6]

Thus, in this psalm, David is not calling down God's vengeance upon transient transgressors of God's laws, who harm out of ignorance or whose abuses are casual rather than premeditated and repetitive. David is condemning those who chronically and violently flaunt their position, contrary to God's righteousness. In particular, its cry resounds against those in positions of governing, legislative, or judicial authority, who exploit their power for evil and their own ends.

Voice of Faith

Moreover, in light of this sustained reality of surrounding societal injustice, Psalm 58 functions as the voice of faith responding to an implied barrage of pointed questions—whether from the psalmist himself or from others to the psalmist. These questions strike at the very heart of faith:

- Is there really a sovereign God who executes justice on this earth?
- Does it make any sense for the righteous still to trust in him when, by all appearances, evil goes unpunished and uncontested?

Indeed, "the foundational principles of existence are on trial."[7] As John Piper passionately says, if God were never to bring vengeance on his enemies and the oppressors of his people,

> then he is an unfaithful God whose covenant is worthless. For he would be saying in effect that it is a matter of complete indifference whether one trusts in him or not. He would be discounting the greatness and worthiness of his own name by admitting that faith and blasphemy are for him as good as equal. Or even worse, he would be awarding blasphemy the greater portion.[8]

It is against just such a background as this that the joy of the righteous must be understood. The righteous rejoice when God comes in vengeance to break the rule of the wicked and to punish injustice. By restoring justice, God will put to rest all doubts and questions. It is the joy and the eternal relief of heaven and God's people to see the liberation of saints, the restoration of justice, and the acquittal of God.[9]

This joy of God's people over the destruction of God's enemies is a motif that runs through the canon of Scripture in like language and imagery. It begins in the Song of Moses (Deut. 32:43), finds expression in the Psalms (58:10), is proclaimed in the Prophets (Jer. 51:48, against literal Babylon), and reaches a climax in the book of Revelation (18:20, against antitypical Babylon).

Intensity of Imagery

But one may ask, "What about the intensity of the imagery? How could the psalmist pray in such hideous terms?" Without doubt, this psalm—and verse 10 in particular—"is one of the most fearful passages in the Old Testament. The combination of vengeance, joy and bloody foot-bath all in one text causes an intuitive aversion."[10] In response to this query, it must be recognized that what is voiced here is poetry. Vivid imagery is inherent in the nature of poetry. Where a concept in narrative may be described dispassionately, in poetry it is more likely to be expressed emotively.

Further, the ancient Semites tended to speak in terms that the modern Western world might phrase more delicately. The Old Testament freely uses the word *hate* to denote both rejection and the negative passion[11] (cf. the various nuances in such passages as Ps. 139:21–22; Hos. 9:15; Mal. 1:2–3). Bloody terminology is found here and throughout eschatological literature. It seems offensive to modern ears to say that "he will bathe his feet in the blood of the wicked" (Ps. 58:10). This language "simply intends to employ a powerful image, borrowed from the all too realistic situation of the battlefield following the fight (wading through the blood), to highlight the total destruction of the godless."[12] Also, much of Scripture's "immoderate" language is heard from the lips of Jesus himself, so that from the perspective of faith, such language may not be unduly—if at all—slighted. And lest one think that Christ merely accommodated his tone to that of a more savage age, it is instructive to note that the Christian canon closes with similar language (e.g., Rev. 14:19–20; 18:4–8, 20; 19:1–3, 15). There, John was using the tongue of the more "rational" Greek culture.

It must be realized that passionate rhetoric naturally and rightly arises from extreme circumstances. "The words wrung from these sufferers as they plead their case are a measure of the deeds which provoked them. Those deeds were not wrung from anyone: they were the brutal response to love (109:4) and to pathetic weakness (137)."[13] Here in Psalm 58, the invectives, hurled one upon the other, express the psalmist's sincere desire as well as his sense of outrage at the flagrant violations of justice.[14] These sentiments must be uttered with passion.

This passion is conveyed by the free use of potent simile, metaphor, and even limited hyperbole. In Psalm 58:6–7, David pleads for Yahweh to break the power of the wicked "gods" or judges. In verses 8–9, he further seeks their sudden demise. And in verse 10, his confidence in Yahweh's intervention of vengeance is depicted by the image of total victory in battle.

In its fiery outbursts, this psalm "fights for the indispensable union of religion and ethics,"[15] the intertwined embrace of life and faith.

Summary and Application

In Psalm 58, David addresses the rulers of the community, ironically labeling them "gods," to inquire whether they do indeed rightly fulfill their judicial function. He responds to his own query with a resounding "No" (vv. 1–2), after which he describes the character of these rulers as wholly wicked and injurious (vv. 3–5). Verses 6–9 comprise the curses that mark the psalm as imprecatory. With vivid imagery and simile, David appeals to Yahweh to render these unjust rulers powerless—and to destroy them if need be. The realization of this longed-for divine vengeance will serve both to vindicate and comfort the righteous who have suffered so grievously. His retribution will establish Yahweh as the manifest and supreme Judge of the earth (vv. 10–11). For with the prevalence of such societal evil, the honor of God and the survival of his faithful are at stake.

In this regard, Calvin's insights are instructive. Reflecting on Psalm 58:10, Calvin comments that, patterned after the example of God, the righteous should

> anxiously desire the conversion of their enemies, and evince much patience under injury, with a view to reclaim them to the way of salvation: but when wilful obstinacy has at last brought round the hour of retribution, it is only natural that they should rejoice to see it inflicted, as proving the interest which God feels in their personal safety.[16]

Although he is generally hesitant to promote the utterance of imprecation, Calvin does affirm its appropriateness on extreme occasions. Commenting on Psalm 109:16, for example, he advises that, since

> we cannot distinguish between the elect and the reprobate, it is our duty to pray for all who trouble us; to desire the salvation of all men; and even to be careful for the welfare of every individual. At the same time, if our hearts are pure and peaceful, this will not prevent us from freely appealing to God's judgment, that he may cut off the finally impenitent.[17]

Christians are indeed called to pray "for kings and all those in authority, that we might lead peaceful and quiet lives in all godliness and propriety" (1 Tim. 2:2). Obedience to this dictum may come to include imprecations like those contained in Psalm 58 if repeated pleas for the establishment of peace and godliness go unanswered. Indeed, the venom of this psalm is reserved for those who, when they should be protecting the helpless under their care, instead persecute and prey upon them.[18] For such as these, even Jesus reserved the harshest sentence. Speaking against the religious leaders of his day, he warned, "Watch out for the scribes . . . who devour the houses of widows! Such will receive the severest judgment" (Mark 12:38, 40).

It is important to note, however, that in Psalm 58 David himself is not seeking to exact revenge—he appeals to the God of vengeance. As Dietrich Bonhoeffer observes, "Whoever entrusts revenge to God dismisses any thought of ever taking revenge himself."[19] So also must it be with all who would seek to image him.

The application of this psalm is directed against governmental and judicial tyranny. Relating this psalm to the modern context of the protected practice of abortion, James Adams reflects: "Millions of unborn babies are put to death in America while the judges of this world keep silent. No, worse than that, they actually justify (in their own minds, at least) the killing of the unborn as an exercise of American liberty. They speak a biased word against justice. They call good what God calls evil."[20] In addition, Bonhoeffer himself took an active stand against the nationalist church under Nazi rule and even participated in an attempt to assassinate Hitler. For him, this had become the *ethical* thing to do in the face of such horrible abuse and unmitigated suffering. This informs for us, as well, when it is "the time to curse."

Theological Foundation:
The Promise of Divine Vengeance

The Song of Moses

Torah (Genesis–Deuteronomy) is the foundational revelation of God—not only because it was given first, but also because in it lies latent, and in germinal form, the expanse of theology that developed thereafter. It is no surprise, then, that the imprecatory psalms base their theology of imprecation in Torah. Indeed, the foundations for imprecation come most notably from (1) the promise of divine vengeance in the

Song of Moses (Deut. 32:1–43), (2) the principle of divine justice in the *lex talionis* (e.g., 19:16–21), and (3) the promise of divine cursing in the Abrahamic covenant (Gen. 12:2–3).

Imprecations in the Psalms are fundamentally cries for God's vengeance to fall upon the stubborn enemies of God and his people. And here in Psalm 58 particularly, as in others,[21] the principal basis upon which David utters his heated cries is this covenantal promise of divine vengeance. This theology of divine vengeance promised to God's people in their distress is given its initial and most classic articulation in Deuteronomy 32—the song of rehearsal and remembrance for God's people, the "Song of Moses."

The book of Deuteronomy is structured after the pattern of ancient suzerain-vassal treaties and, in keeping with this form, Deuteronomy 32:1–43 functions as a "witness" of the covenant. This characterization of the Song of Moses is underscored by its intended use as literature that would be repeatedly sung in the lives of God's people.[22]

Moreover, the Song of Moses has an ongoing prophetic function. It is a witness to the ongoing covenant of God with his people—the application of which carries through to the end of the canon. Through the canon, the cry for divine vengeance for the blood of saints is raised until Revelation 6:9–10, and in 19:1–2, those gathered around the throne rejoice in its accomplishment. This prophetic nature illustrates both the primary and secondary purposes of the Song. It is primarily a witness against Israel for their rebellions (cf. Deut. 31:19–21, 28; 32:5–30). Secondarily it is a testimony to the faithfulness of God in the face of his people's faithlessness, including his faithfulness in taking vengeance against oppressors (cf. Deut. 32:4, 31–43).[23]

The most relevant part of the text for this discussion is Deuteronomy 32:33–43:

> [33]Their [i.e., the heathen oppressors'][24] wine is the venom of serpents,
>   the cruel poison of cobras.
> [34]. . . . .
> [35]Vengeance is mine, I will repay.
>   In due time their [i.e., the oppressors'] foot will slip;
> for the day of their disaster is near
>   and their doom comes swiftly.

[36]Surely, Yahweh will judge[25] his people
    and have compassion on his servants
when he sees that their power is gone
    and none remains—bond or free.
[37]Then he will say, "Where are their [i.e., his rebellious people's] gods,
    the rock in whom they took refuge?
[38] . . . .
[39]See now that I, I am he,
    and there are no gods besides me.
I put to death and I bring to life,
    I have wounded and I will heal,
    and no one can deliver out of my hand.
[40]Surely, I lift my hand to heaven
    and declare: As I live forever,
[41]when I sharpen my flashing sword
    and my hand grasps it in judgment,
I will take vengeance on my adversaries
    and repay those who hate me.
[42]I will make my arrows drunk with blood
    and my sword will devour flesh—
drunk with the blood of the slain and the captives,
    with the long-haired heads of the enemy."
[43]Rejoice, O nations, with his people,
    and let all the "gods" worship him.[26]
Surely, the blood of his servants he will avenge;
    he will take vengeance on his adversaries
    and make atonement for the land of his people.

Likely Allusion

At several points, Psalm 58 likely alludes to the latter half of the Song of Moses as the literary and theological quarry from which the content of its cry is mined. First, the psalm arose out of a faith context and was to be used in the worshiping community. Thus, the divine vengeance itself, so earnestly longed for, must have been addressed in prior revelation in such a manner as to convey that the righteous might expect such from their covenant God. And from the temporal standpoint of David, the consummate articulation of this promised divine vengeance is found in Deuteronomy 32.

Second, the social context out of which the psalmist speaks is that of powerlessness in the face of oppression, and he cries out in confidence to the God who can indeed act decisively on behalf of his defeated people. This very element runs strongly through the final verses of the Song of Moses: when all the power (literally "hand,") of his rebellious people is gone because of their heathen oppressors (Deut. 32:36), God demonstrates the power of his hand, from which none can deliver (v. 39). He lifts it to heaven with a self-imposed oath (v. 40), and grasps his sword with his hand to wreak vengeance on his enemies (v. 41).

Third, although a consistently precise terminology cannot be identified, a similarity of language and linkage of concepts is conspicuous between the two passages. It is probable that the psalmist was not only aware of the Song as he uttered his cry, but he subtly invoked its promise.

In Psalm 58, David taunts the unjust "gods" (v. 1), asserting that, indeed, "there is a God" who judges (v. 11). Likewise in Deuteronomy 32, Yahweh taunts the pagan gods (v. 37), asserting that "there are no gods" except him (v. 39). He is the God of justice (v. 4).

In Psalm 58, David compares the wicked oppressors[27] to venomous snakes, and deaf cobras (v. 4).[28] In Deuteronomy 32, Yahweh associates the persecutors of his people with the imagery of venomous serpents and deadly cobras (v. 33).

In Psalm 58:10, bloody vengeance is longed for. In Deuteronomy 32:41–43 that graphically bloody vengeance is promised, and in the hope of vengeance realized, the righteous rejoice (Ps. 58:10; Deut. 32:43).

Other imprecatory psalms hark back to the language and imagery of the latter part of this Song as the theological foundation and justification for cries for vengeance. Psalm 94 begins with an appeal to the "God of vengeance" to repay the evil oppressors (vv. 1–2). Even more germane, and most overt in its allusion to Deuteronomy 32, is Psalm 79. Uttered out of a context of community desolation, it is truly a crisis of life and faith. After laying before Yahweh Israel's hopeless and helpless situation, the psalmist locates the cause of their calamities in the anger and jealousy of Yahweh against his "inheritance" for their sins (vv. 5, 8). He then pleads for compassion and forgiveness (vv. 8–9) and for the outpouring of divine wrath instead on the ungodly nations who have wreaked such havoc (vv. 6–7).

This pattern is found in Deuteronomy 32. In verses 21–22, Yahweh is provoked to jealousy and anger against his "inheritance" by their stubborn rebellions against him. Out of this jealous wrath, Yahweh promises to send various evils against them, including the ravages of the nations (vv. 23–33). But at the point of Israel's powerlessness, Yahweh promises compassion, vindication, and vengeance (vv. 34–43).

Psalm 79:10, however, makes the most explicit comparison. It pointedly requests of Yahweh that "the avenging of the outpoured blood of your servants" be known among the nations. This is the promise of Deuteronomy 32:43, which calls on the nations to rejoice, for Yahweh "avenges the blood of his servants."

Continuing Song

Far from being an isolated and peripheral portion of Old Testament biblical theology, the promise of divine vengeance in Deuteronomy 32 is central to the theology and hope of all Scripture. It is carried from the Law through the Prophets[29] and the Psalms to the end of the canon. Indeed, verse 35 is quoted by the apostle Paul in Romans 12:19 in his justification of New Testament ethics.

In addition, in Revelation 6:9–11, both the cry of the saints in heaven for this vengeance and the context out of which they cry—their martyrdom—bluntly recall the promise of God in the latter portion of the Song of Moses to "avenge the blood of his servants" (Deut. 32:43). Revelation 6:9–11 proclaims,

> [9]And when he opened the fifth seal, I saw under the altar the souls of those who had been slaughtered because of the word of God and the testimony they held on to. [10]They called out in a loud voice, "How long, O Master, holy and true, until you judge the inhabitants of the earth and avenge our blood?" [11]Then each of them was given a white robe, and they were told to wait yet a

little longer, until (the number of) their fellow servants and brothers who were about to be killed, as they had been, was completed.

This eschatological tie is explicit in Revelation 15:2–4. At the close of the ages and following the bloody vengeance described in Revelation 14:19–20, the saints in glory sing "the *Song of Moses*[30] and the Song of the Lamb" (15:3, emphasis added)—a song that proclaims the greatness of God's justice revealed, and the consequent worship to arise from the nations (cf. Deut. 32:43). According to Revelation 15:2–4,

> [2]And I saw . . . those who had been victorious over the beast and over his image and over the number of his name . . . holding harps (given them) by God. [3]And they were singing the Song of Moses the servant of God and the Song of the Lamb:
>
> > "Great and marvelous are your works,
> >   O Lord God Almighty.
> > Just and true are your ways,
> >   O King of the nations.
> > [4]Who does not (now) fear (you), O Lord,
> >   and glorify your name,
> >   who alone is holy?
> > All the nations will come
> >   and worship before you,
> >   for your judgments have been revealed."

Amid the extended judgments—those that occur against eschatological Babylon, reminiscent of Jeremiah 51:48—comes the call to "rejoice" at this execution of divine retribution (Rev. 18:20; cf. Deut. 32:43).

The Song of Moses is sung in a covenant context, and the promise of vengeance is founded upon God's having entered into covenant with his people. Although the Song of Moses was intended fundamentally to be a "witness against" Israel upon her breach of covenant with Yahweh (Deut. 31:19, 21, 28), it was also a song of hope (32:36, 43). It declares that Yahweh will not abandon his people regardless of their faithlessness. He will come to their aid, avenge their blood, and take vengeance on his enemies.[31] The cry for vengeance, then, arises out of this context and appeals to the terms of the covenant. The terms include this promise of vengeance against the enemies of God and his people—a promise applicable not solely to the Israel of the old covenant but also to the inheritors of the new covenant, as affirmed by Revelation 6:10.[32]

Four

Baby Bashing: Psalm 137

Curse Against a National or Community Enemy

[1]By the rivers of Babylon,
    there we sat and we wept,
    when we remembered Zion.
[2]On the poplars in her midst
    we hung our lyres.
[3]For there they demanded of us—
    our captors, song;
    and our slave-drivers, mirth:
    "Sing for us one of the songs of Zion!"
[4]How can we sing Yahweh's song
    on foreign soil?
[5]If I forget you, O Jerusalem,
    may my right hand forget . . . ![1]
[6]May my tongue cling to my palate
    if I do not remember you,
if I do not lift up Jerusalem
    as my chief joy.
[7]Remember, O Yahweh, against the Edomites—
    the day of Jerusalem!
They cried, "Raze her, raze her—
    down to her foundation!"

[8]O Daughter of Babylon, (doomed to be) devastated,
   blessed is he who repays you
      what you deserve for what you did to us!
[9]Blessed is he who seizes and shatters
   your little ones against the cliff![2]

—Psalm 137

Common Objections

The beautifully crafted—yet disturbing—Psalm 137 has been under-standably dubbed "the 'psalm of violence' par excellence, and, at least in its full text, to be rejected by Christians."[3] For have not Christians been schooled in the law of Christ to "love your enemies, do good to those who hate you, bless those who curse you, pray for those who mistreat you," and "turn the other cheek" (Luke 6:27–29)? And have they not been steeped in his words from the cross, the height of human cruelty and maltreatment—"Father, forgive them" (23:34)? The words of Psalm 137:8–9 in particular have been coined "the ironical 'bitter beatitudes,'" the sentiment of which is "the very reverse of true religion," and "among the most repellant words in scripture."[4] They are called a frightfully cruel outcry of "blind hate and vulgar rage."[5]

Many Christians of a supposedly milder age, scandalized by such a wish contained therein, have jettisoned the last three verses of this psalm from the worship of the church and the life of the faithful altogether. This solution runs counter to the usefulness and inspiration of Scrip-ture.[6] Others of like mind have sought to salvage these verses by relegating them to that age before the Cross—now antithetical to what Christians are called to be. John Bright, for example, claims that the composer of Psalm 137 "is typical of that man in every age who is godly and devoted to the things of God," yet who responds "from a pre-Christian perspec-tive and in a not-yet-Christian spirit." To such a man, Bright avers, "the gospel must come as a strange thing. We know this man well: there is more than a little of him in most of us."[7]

An alternative perception attempts to maintain the psalmist's piety (and that of all the later faithful who would—even haltingly—echo these words) and yet avoids the inherent violence in the text, by urging an allegorical interpretation of these words. C. S. Lewis, for instance, has mused,

> Of the cursing Psalms, I suppose most of us make our own moral allegories. . . . We know the proper object of utter hostility—wickedness, especially our own. . . . From this point of view I can use even the horrible passage in 137 about dashing the Babylonian babies against the stones. I know things in the inner world which are like babies; the infantile beginnings of small indulgences, small resentments, which may one day become dipsomania or settled hatred, but which woo us and wheedle us with special pleadings and seem so tiny, so helpless that in resisting them we feel we are being cruel to animals. They begin whimpering to us "I don't ask much, but", or "I had at least hoped", or "you owe yourself *some* consideration". Against all such pretty infants (the dears have such winning ways) the advice of the Psalm is the best. Knock the little bastards' brains out. And "blessed" is he who can, for it's easier said than done.[8]

In a more corporeal vein, Howard Osgood sought to remove the offense of Psalm 137:8–9 by arguing that the Hebrew term for "your little ones" referred more to relationship than to age, and so viewed the "children" of Babylon as her adult progeny who chose and followed in her sins.[9]

Historical Context

Noble (and poignant) though these sentiments are, the psalm in light of its historical context lends itself to an understanding contrary to the "higher morality" and "allegorical" interpretations common in Western Christianity. This communal lament is sung from the context of the Babylonian exile—an exile preceded by the unthinkable horrors of ancient siege warfare and the "day" of Jerusalem's destruction. Jerusalem's demise at the hands of the pitiless Babylonians, goaded on by the treacherous Edomites (cf. Obad. 10–16; Ezek. 35:5–6), was a national atrocity that virtually wiped out and deported the community of faith. Moreover, in Jerusalem's demise were destroyed the bastions of that faith: the Davidic monarch, the chosen city, and the temple of God. All those things that had rooted Israel's identity as a nation and—more specifically—as the people of God had been either demolished or uprooted.

Siege warfare in the ancient Near East was frighteningly cruel.[10] In the Vassal-treaties of Esarhaddon, in fact, many of the consequences promised in the event of covenant disloyalty bespeak these horrors of the siege:

> May Shamash plow up your cities with an iron plow.
> Just as this ewe is cut open and the flesh of its young placed in its mouth, so may he [Shamash?] make you eat in your hunger the flesh of your brothers, your sons, and your daughters.
> . . . .
> Just as honey is sweet, so may the blood of your women, your sons and daughters taste sweet in your mouths.
> . . . .
> Just as honeycomb is pierced through and through with holes, so may holes be pierced through and through in your flesh, the flesh of your women, your brothers, your sons and daughters while you are alive.[11]

In addition to these cruelties, the most brutal—and all-too-common—practice of city conquerors was the killing of infants inside the womb or the dashing of infants against the rocks in the fury and totality of war's carnage.[12] This barbarous slaughter of the most helpless noncombatants "effected total destruction by making war upon the next generation."[13] The Scriptures make further use of this graphic and gruesome picture in its judgment oracles against rebellious Israel (Hos. 13:16), Jerusalem (Luke 19:44), and cruel Assyria (Nah. 3:10).

Most notably here, it is a fate promised to Babylon (Isa. 13:16).

Force of the Appeal

Tormented by "the harsh, pitiless slave-drivers who drove the prisoners they had plundered hundreds of miles eastward to distant Babylon,"[14] the abrupt and appalling shriek emanating from Psalm 137:7–9 is, then, the "passionate outcry of the powerless demanding justice!"[15] Indeed, in the face of such blatant and humanly unpunishable injustice, God's chastised people had no other recourse but to turn to Yahweh and plead for his justice. In the midst of their helplessness and humiliation, he was "their only hope for a righteous and just sentence of condemnation."[16] And it is to him that their appeal for strict retaliation in both kind and degree is made—and surrendered.[17]

But does even this context prepare us for, or justify, the sentiment expressed in the emotional climax of the psalm? These latter verses, indeed, raise that profound question with which the faithful of both Testaments must surely grapple: How could the supposedly pious psalmist ring out a cry for such violence and revenge that he would call "blessed" those who pick up the enemy's infants and dash them mercilessly against the rocks—a death none ought lightly to visualize?

Theological Foundation:
The Principle of Divine Justice

Just Recompense

The basis upon which the psalmist pleads for such horrid retribution, although interlaced with extreme emotion, is not the base and vicious fury of bloodthirsty revenge but the principle of divine justice itself, particularly as expressed in the so-called *lex talionis* (eye for an eye, tooth for a tooth). It is stated three times in Torah—the seedbed of all subsequent theology (cf. Exod. 21:22–25; Lev. 24:17–22; Deut. 19:16–21). Rather than serving as a sanction for personal vengeance, this Old Testament command actually protected against excesses of revenge. Essentially, it was designed to ensure justice: the punishment would indeed fit the crime.

Thus, rather than being a primitive and barbaric code, this Old Testament statute forms the basis for all civilized justice. It was not a law of private retaliation, but a law of just recompense. Indeed, Gordon Wenham observes with insight that *eye for an eye* was likely just a governing formula for dispensing justice:

In most cases in Israel it was not applied literally. It meant that compensation appropriate to the loss incurred must be paid out. Thus if a slave lost an eye, he was given his freedom (Exod. 21:26). The man who killed an ox had to pay its owner enough for him to buy another (Lev. 24:18). Only in the case of premeditated murder was such compensation forbidden (Num. 35:16ff.). Then the principle of *life for life* must be literally enforced, because man is made in the image of God (Genesis 9:5–6).[18]

Lex Talionis

Definition: "the law [lex] of retaliation." The *lex talionis* is a law of equal and direct retribution: "an eye for an eye, a tooth for a tooth, a life for a life."

References in Pentateuch: Exodus 21:22–25; Leviticus 24:17–22; Deuteronomy 19:16–21

New Testament Instances: Paul's curse of Elymas the sorcerer (Acts 13:6-12); Paul's denunciation of antagonist Alexander (2 Tim. 4:14); downfall of eschatological Babylon (Rev. 18:6, 20).

By Jesus' day, and contrary to its intent, the *lex talionis* had indeed become a "law of retaliation," sanctioning a mind-set of revenge rendered by the phrase, "Do unto others as they have done unto you." Jesus' words in Matthew 5:38–42, however, were given to shock his followers back to a recovery of the original intent of the law (cf. v. 17), not by explaining its proper use, but by prohibiting its perversion. That means setting aside "rights" of private retaliation and nurturing an attitude of long-suffering.[19]

Judicial Context

The intended implementation of this *lex talionis*, according to the evidence of the Old Testament Scriptures, was in a judicial, rather than a personal, context. Deuteronomy 19:16–21 makes this most explicit (emphasis added):

> [16]If a malevolent witness should rise up against a man to accuse him of a crime, [17]then the two men involved in the dispute are to stand *before Yahweh, before the priests and the judges* who are in office at the time. [18]Then *the judges* are to investigate the matter completely, and if the witness is found to be a false witness, falsely accusing his brother, [19]then you are to do to him as he intended to do to his brother, and so you will purge the evil from your midst. [20]The rest will hear and be afraid, and never again will this evil thing be done in your midst. [21]Your eye must show no pity: life for life, eye for eye, tooth for tooth, hand for hand, foot for foot.

In Leviticus 24:17–21, the *lex talionis* in expanded form is nestled within a pericope (vv. 10–23) in which appropriate judgment for blasphemy was placed before Yahweh, and the people awaited his sentence. The divine verdict then forms the stage from which Yahweh reiterated the principle of justice by which his people were to be governed. That principle had first been uttered in Exodus 21:22–25. Even there, the punishment for personal injury was to be placed before both the wronged party and "the judges" for appropriate judgment (v. 22). And as the canon continued, the restriction on personal—as opposed to judicial—retaliation was made even more explicit. Indeed, it was as strictly forbidden in the Mosaic economy as in the words of Jesus. Proverbs 24:29 warns, "Do not say, 'Just as he did to me, so I will do to him; I will pay that man back for what he has done'" (cf. 20:22). Jesus himself likewise summed up the Law and the Prophets in words reminiscent of these: "In all things, then, whatever you would like people to do to you, so also you do to them" (Matt. 7:12).

Not only did God institute the *lex talionis* in the law code of Israel, but "it was a law which was, in fact, based upon the very *nature* of God. Yahweh, although a God of love, is also a God of retribution who deals with his creature's trespasses against his holiness on the basis of his retributive justice."[20] This is seen most clearly and poignantly in the necessity for the Cross. And it is the Cross that both bridges and binds the two testaments.

Since it is a grounding assertion that the nature of God does not change (cf. Mal. 3:6; Heb. 13:8), the principle of divine justice based on that nature, as encased in the judicial *lex talionis*, must remain fundamentally constant.[21] So, too, the implication lingers that the appeal to this principle may still find its legitimate place. [22]

Prophetic Awareness

When the psalmist uttered his impassioned plea, he was evidently familiar with the prophecy of Jeremiah 50–51 and had taken its promise of divine retribution to heart. This tie is most pronounced in the comparison between Psalm 137:8 and Jeremiah 51:56, for in both instances the terms for *devastate*, *repay*, and *recompense* occur together[23] in relation to the expected judgment against brutal Babylon:

> O Daughter of Babylon, (doomed to be) devastated,
>> blessed is he who repays you
>>> what you deserve for what you did to us! (Ps. 137:8)

> Indeed, a devastator will come against Babylon, . . .
> For Yahweh is a God of recompense;
>> he will surely repay! (Jer. 51:56)

This psalm is as much a response to Scripture as it is to events.[24] Other striking parallels occur:

- The designation "Daughter of Babylon" (compare Jer. 50:42; 51:33 with Ps. 137:8);
- The depiction of Babylon dying after being rolled off the cliffs. The invincible destroying mountain will soon be no more (compare Jer. 51:25 with Ps. 137:9);
- Ironic use of the violent term *shatter* (נָפַץ, *nāpaṣ*). Babylon once was used by Yahweh to "shatter" the nations. But this government will soon see her own little ones "shattered" (compare its repeated use in Jer. 51:20–23 with Ps. 137:9).

In addition, Jeremiah 50–51 skillfully weaves together the twin themes of the promise of divine vengeance and the principle of divine justice—or the promise of vengeance in kind.[25] The former is classically expressed in the Song of Moses[26] (Deut. 32:35), the latter in the *lex talionis*. And this dual-edged promise is encapsulated in Jeremiah 51:6: "For it is the time of Yahweh's vengeance; he will repay her what she deserves!" This text finds echo not only in Psalm 137:7–9, but also in that other communal imprecatory prayer—Psalm 79:10, 12.[27]

Summary and Tension

Psalm 137 arises out of a context of absolute devastation, anguish, and hopelessness—except in the faint yet tenacious faith in the covenant God. Thus, in verses 7–9 the psalmist appeals to Yahweh for recompense against the treacherous Edomites and the merciless Babylonians—utter destruction as depicted by, and actually enacted in, the violent slaughter of the enemy's infants. The cry is for a punishment commensurate with the crime committed. Here the crime was the height of barbarity and ought be repaid in kind. In such a circumstance, "a feeling of universal love is admirable, but it must not be divorced from a keen sense of justice."[28] The plea is made to Yahweh to fulfill justice as expressed in the *lex talionis*. Whatever army is used to exact punishment will be "blessed."

Through such a tool, justice will be realized, the honor of God will be upheld, and a certain measure of the world gone wrong will be righted. Such matters as these are not to be received by the righteous with regret but with a measure of rejoicing, albeit perhaps somber rejoicing.

This very measure of rejoicing is, at the culmination of the New Testament canon, *commanded* of both heaven and God's saints over the future devastation of antitypical Babylon, that demonstration being the ultimate realization of the psalmist's cry. This future devastation follows the requirements of the *lex talionis*: "Give back to her just as she has given, and pay her back double for what she has done. . . . Rejoice over her, O heaven and saints and apostles and prophets! For God has judged her for the way she treated you" (Rev. 18:6, 20).[29]

But the question may yet be asked whether the psalmist's appeal to the *lex talionis* was legitimate. The question seems particularly relevant in light of God's command that children not be put to death for the sins of their fathers (Deut. 24:16). If the cry of the psalmist had been merely for repayment, the nature of which was left unspecified, there would probably be minimal objection to the psalm. The offense comes because this is an explicit and seemingly barbaric request.[30]

In response, it must be noted that Deuteronomy 24:16 refers to a judicial sentence that is to be carried out by men. God retains the prerogative to visit the iniquity of the fathers upon the children (Exod. 34:7). The most conspicuous example of this is when, after God's long-suffering over their sin, he commanded the annihilation of the entire populace of Canaan as his people entered their inheritance there. God has rights that man cannot have, for only he is God. Harsh and revolting though his justice may appear, the believer is called to trust God's goodness, even in the midst of his justice, and accept any concomitant tensions.

Thus, in line with ethical standards,[31] Psalm 137:7–9 appeals to Yahweh as the Judge supreme to mete out justice according to his own edict. And since, in God's economy, no ransom was to be allowed for murder (cf. Num. 35:31), the psalmist cries out for the divine judgment of compensatory bloodshed. Modern people in particular are shocked and horrified by this appalling request—rightly so, for it scales the reaches of revulsion—yet it falls within the bounds of divine jurisprudence. This sentence is both divinely promised (cf. Isa. 13:16; Jer. 50–51) and divinely enacted. Thus, the principle of strict judicial retaliation cannot be maligned without maligning the character of God, who both established and promised it.

As such, then, the psalmist bears no guilt for his cry, though its jarring effect—and even its scarring—remains.

The Lex Talionis Today

But is this a cry that Christians can legitimately and in good conscience echo in their lives and worship? After all, Psalm 137 was considered worthy to be retained in the book of worship for God's people of the old covenant and was embraced into the canon of the New Testament church. Although Leslie C. Allen insists that the "Christian faith teaches a new way, the pursuit of forgiveness and a call to love," he asks with perception, "Yet is there forgiveness for a Judas (cf. John 17:12) or for the Antichrist?"[32] Edom and Babylon were the ancient examples of "Antichrist," as were Judas and the false teachers in the early church. There may come times in which the modern church, the present expression of the people of God, may join with her brothers and sisters of past ages and appeal for the devastation of a current manifestation of "Antichrist." If so, they should use language appropriate to the offense.

In saying this, it is understood today, as it was in the time of the psalmist, that the enactment of such an expression of bitter grief and anger is left entirely in the hands of God. Leaving the matter with God, the person abandons any personal desire for revenge. Yet, whether at any moment one is able to legitimately echo these words for oneself, they may, it would seem, be offered for fellow brothers and sisters who are victims of widespread rape, murder, mutilation, and enslavement at the hands of a wicked regime. This is particularly so when none is willing or able to assist.

This has been the circumstance in Sudan in recent years, in the Islamic government's appalling program of genocide against the Christian population. Similar violent atrocities are standard procedure for terrorist organizations like Al Qaeda, whose leader, Bin Laden, was the mastermind behind the September 11, 2001 attacks on the United States. And his subordinate, Zarqawi, continues to direct the terrorist bombings and brutal beheadings of noncombatants in Iraq.

In such circumstances of real, horrible brutality like that addressed by the psalmist, where there is the pressing temptation to "forget" or abandon the faith for the sake of self-protection (cf. Ps. 137:5–6), this psalm explodes upward. It turns over the matter of justice to the Source of power in the midst of powerlessness, of hope in the midst of hopelessness. As such a need arises, "may God give His church the courage to be so bold."[33]

Five

Unholy Litany: Psalm 109

Curse Against a Personal Enemy

[1]For the director of music;[1] a psalm of David.

O God whom I praise, do not be silent!
[2]For the mouth of the wicked and the mouth of the treacherous
    have opened against me;
      they have spoken against me with deceitful tongues.
[3]With words of hatred they have surrounded me,
    and have attacked me without cause.
[4]In return for my love they accuse me,
    though I continue to pray (for them).[2]
[5]They repay me evil for good,
    and hatred for my love.
[6]Appoint a wicked man against him,
    and let an accuser stand at his right hand![3]
[7]When he is tried, let him be found guilty,
    and let his plea be considered as sin.
[8]May his days be few;
    may another take his office.
[9]May his children be fatherless
    and his wife a widow.
[10]May his children wander about and beg,
    and may they be driven from their ruined homes.

¹¹May a creditor seize all that he has,
     and may strangers plunder what he has gained from his labor.
¹²Let there be no one to extend loving-kindness to him,
     nor to take pity on his fatherless children.
¹³May his descendants be cut off;
     may their name be blotted out in the next generation.
¹⁴May the iniquity of his fathers be remembered before Yahweh,
     and may the sin of his mother never be blotted out.
¹⁵May they remain before Yahweh continually,
     and may he cut off their memory from the earth.
¹⁶For he never remembered to show loving-kindness,
     but persecuted the poor and needy
     and disheartened to their death.
¹⁷He loved cursing—so may it come on him;
     and he found no pleasure in blessing—so may it be far from
     him.⁴
¹⁸He clothed himself with cursing as his coat;
     so may it enter into his body like water
     and into his bones like oil.
¹⁹May it be like a cloak wrapped about him,
     and like a belt tied forever around him.
²⁰May this be⁵ Yahweh's payment to my accusers,
     even to those who speak evil against my life.
²¹But you, O Yahweh my Lord,
     deal with me according to your name;⁶
     because your loving-kindness is so good, deliver me.
²²For I am poor and needy,
     and my heart is pierced within me.
²³Like a lengthening shadow, I fade away;
     I am shaken off like a locust.
²⁴My knees give way from fasting,
     and my body has lost all its fat.
²⁵I have become an object of reproach to them;
     when they see me, they shake their heads.
²⁶Help me, O Yahweh my God;
     save me according to your loving-kindness.

²⁷And let them know that this is your hand—
    that you, O Yahweh, have done it.
²⁸Let them curse, but may you bless;
        may those who rise up against me be put to shame,
        but may your servant rejoice.
²⁹May my accusers be clothed with disgrace,
        and may they be wrapped in their own shame as in a robe.
³⁰With my mouth I will greatly extol Yahweh;
        and in the midst of the multitude I will praise him.
³¹For he stands at the right hand of the needy,
        to save his life from those who would condemn him.
                                            —Psalm 109

Above all other psalms of imprecation, this cascade of curse upon curse has been reproached as, for example, "the 'imprecatory' psalm *par excellence*,"[7] a "pregnant missile of evil,"[8] a "raw undisciplined song of hate,"[9] and "as unabashed a hymn of hate as was ever written."[10] Evidence certainly supports such descriptions. Without question, "this is one of the hard places of Scripture, a passage the soul trembles to read."[11] This yearning for precise, appalling retaliation confronts Christians with an enigma. It seems a vivid contradiction of those calls to "love your enemies" (Matt. 5:44) and to "bless, and curse not" (Rom. 12:14).

Indeed, David imprecates his enemy in a manner starkly reminiscent of certain ancient Near East curse formulas. Compare Psalm 109:8, "May his days be few," with the curse of Esarhaddon, "May he never grant you . . . attainment of old age."[12] Furthermore, this psalm has been sorely misused in the life of the broader Christian community. Calvin records, for instance, that a reprehensible abuse of this psalm occurred in his day— the vengeful would pay others to pray someone to death:

How detestable a piece of sacrilege is it on the part of the monks, and especially the Franciscan friars, to pervert this psalm by employing it to countenance the most nefarious purposes! If a man harbour malice against a neighbour, it is quite a common thing for him to engage one of these wicked wretches to curse him, which he would do by daily repeating this psalm. I know a lady in France who hired a parcel of these friars to curse her own and only son in these words.[13]

Whose Cursing?

The initial question that must be asked in regard to Psalm 109 is, "From whose lips do the vehement curses of verses 6–19 escape—David's or his enemy's?" In modern treatments of the psalm, verses 6–19 are often put in quotation marks. They are regarded as the words that David's enemy uttered against him. If this can be demonstrated to be the exegetically preferred interpretation, the offense of the psalm is largely alleviated, and a moral dilemma avoided (although it does nothing to alleviate the offense of the other imprecatory psalms).[14]

Note, however, that a key internal element runs counter to this proposition, that is, the repeated designation "poor and needy" (עָנִי וְאֶבְיוֹן, ʿānî wĕʾebyôn). This is a stock phrase synonymous with the "pious" in the psalms. It is used in Psalm 109:16 and 22 (and thus, both inside and outside the "frame"; cf. v. 31). An intentional verbal and emotional tie appears between the psalmist and the one calling for retribution:

> For he [i.e., the psalmist's enemy] never
> remembered to show loving-kindness,
> but persecuted the poor and needy
> and disheartened to their death. (Psalm 109:16)

> For I [i.e., the psalmist] am poor and needy,
> and my heart is pierced within me. (Psalm 109:22)

A striking parallel to this litany of curses in Psalm 109:6–19 can be seen in Jeremiah 18:19–23. In Jeremiah 18, Yahweh answers the prophet's requests with promised disaster:

> [19]Pay attention to me, Yahweh;
>> listen to the voice of those who contend with me!
> [20]*Should evil be repaid for good?*
>> Yet they have dug a pit for me.

Remember that I stood before you
> to speak well on their behalf,
> to turn your wrath from them.
21Therefore, give their children over to famine;
> and hand them over to the power of the sword.
> *Let their wives be made childless and widows;*
> ....
23But you know, Yahweh,
> all their plots to kill me.
Do not atone for their iniquity
> *or blot out their sin from before you.*
Let them be overthrown before you;
> deal with them in the time of your anger. (emphasis added)

In addition, the apostles understood these to be the words of David rather than his enemy. Peter, concerning Judas Iscariot, explicitly applies the imprecation in Psalm 109:8 as the words of David (Acts 1:16, 20). In Peter's application lies implicit commendation of the initial utterance.[15] Moreover, the typological application of this psalm to that "close associate turned vile betrayer" places the curses of Psalm 109 in their appropriate context and use.

Appeal for Justice

The trespass that spawns the denunciations of David is no petty or transient matter, but rather the return of hatred for his sustained love, of evil for his sustained good (Ps. 109:4–5). This theme is elsewhere repeated in the imprecatory psalms, fleshed out in greater detail. In 35:11–15, 19 (cf. 38:19–20), David likewise recites,

11Malevolent witnesses rise up;
> they question me about things I do not know.
12*They repay me evil for good—*
> what bereavement to my soul!
13Yet I, when they were sick, clothed myself in sackcloth,

I humbled myself in fasting;
    but my prayers returned to me unanswered.
[14]I paced back and forth as though for my friend or brother;
    I bowed my head in grief as though mourning for my mother.
[15]But when I stumbled, they gathered in glee. . . .

. . . .

[19]Let not those rejoice over me
    who are wrongfully my enemies;
let not those who hate me without cause
    (maliciously) wink the eye. (emphasis added)

In Psalm 109, David was in a position of desperate need (cf. vv. 16, 22, 31) and had already shown a pattern of enemy-love. This love, however, had been both spurned and answered with repeated enmity. Moreover, even in the midst of the enemy's litigations and David's counter-imprecations, David apparently continued to show concern for the enemy in his prayers (v. 4).[16] In light of his enemy's appalling lack of loving-kindness,[17] climaxing in the enemy's abuse of the legal system, David resorts to his only remaining recourse.[18] David appeals to the divine Judge of all the earth, who will indeed act justly (cf. Gen. 18:25). He asks in Psalm 109 that the abuse shown by the enemy be returned in full measure according to the demands of the *lex talionis:*[19]

- "For the mouth of the wicked . . . [has] opened against me," verse 2, is answered by verse 6, "Appoint a wicked man against him," and verse 7, "When he is tried, let him be found guilty [lit., wicked]."
- "In return for my love they accuse me," verse 4, is answered by verse 6, "Let an accuser stand at his right hand," and verse 20, "May this be Yahweh's payment to my accusers".
- "He never remembered to show loving-kindness," verse 16, is answered by verse 12, "Let there be no one to extend loving-kindness to him."
- "He . . . persecuted the poor and needy and disheartened to their death," verse 16, is answered by the imprecations that invoke such a state upon the oppressor (vv. 8–15).

- "He loved cursing," verse 17, is answered immediately by "so may it come on him" and throughout verses 17–19. His appeal informs our understanding of the evils of his enemy. Those horrific imprecations wished upon the enemy in verses 8–15 characterize the very crimes the enemy had committed (cf. vv. 16–20).
- "He clothed himself with cursing," verse 18, is countered by the plea in verse 29 that the psalmist's "accusers be clothed with disgrace."

Notice again that, although a known personal enemy[20] is imprecated, David does not react in private revenge, as would be expected in such a circumstance. Rather he releases the retaliatory demands of justice to the God under whose jurisdiction it rightfully lies (cf. Deut. 32:35; Rom. 12:19).[21] He brings his hurt and hurtful cry for vengeance to God (Psalm 109:1, 21, 26–29). And once divine deliverance is realized, this cry will transform to public praise (vv. 30–31).[22]

Such is the nature of God's acts. Vengeance upon his enemies is salvation for his people. God has taken sides in his covenant, and he has bound himself to remain faithful to it.

Theological Foundation:
The Promise of Divine Cursing

The Abrahamic Covenant

But if Psalm 109 is to be construed as the genuine words of David against a personal enemy, how can these vivid and explicit curses be justified—particularly the curse passed down to the offender's children (e.g., Psalm 109:10, 12–15)? In addition to the divine principle expressed in the *lex talionis*, dealt with earlier, the basis upon which David could justifiably call down such terrible curses upon those who had so malevolently treated him was the covenant with Abraham. From the first promises to Abraham in Genesis 12:3, God had said he would curse those who cursed his people.[23]

> I will bless those who bless you,
>> and he who curses you I will curse [וּמְקַלֶּלְךָ אָאֹר,
>> *ûmĕqallelkā ʾāʾôr*].

The Abrahamic covenant, of which this promise is a part, assured divine blessing on those who would bless the "faith-descendants" of Abraham and divine cursing (אָרַר, ʾārar) on those who would treat them with contempt (קָלַל, qālal).[24] For the emphasis in the Abrahamic covenant of Genesis 12:2–3 is not so much on the nation as it is on the people of God.[25] This is made clear not only in Galatians 3:6–29, which asserts that the essence of the Abrahamic covenant embraces the New Testament saint as it did the Old, but also in the threatened curses and grave warnings divinely uttered against the wicked within the covenant community of Israel (e.g., Ps. 50:16–22). The faith, rather than the race, of Abraham is the principal mark of identity (cf. Rom. 2:28–29).[26]

Genesis 12:3 portrays the enemies of God's people as the enemies of God. In Psalm 109, David takes hold of this. In an intense manner he makes appeal to God—in a form familiar in the ancient Near East—to do as he had promised: to curse those who had so mistreated him.[27]

True to His Word

Literary echoes of Genesis 12:3 are found in this psalm. Psalm 109:17 speak of this contemptuous "cursing" of the enemy along with his lack of "blessing." Likewise, and most directly, in verse 28, the enemy's "cursing" (קָלַל, qālal) is contrasted with Yahweh's "blessing."

In addition, distinct allusion to earlier cursing formulas established in the Mosaic covenant—which builds upon the Abrahamic promises—are expressed in David's imprecations. In essence, he is reminding God to be true to his promise to curse—and to curse specifically as he had promised. Psalm 109:9, for instance—"May his children be fatherless and his wife a widow"—makes explicit appeal to talionic justice in harking back to the words of Yahweh in Exodus 22:22–24: "Do not oppress any widow or the fatherless. For if you oppress them and they cry out to me, I will surely hear their cry. Then my anger will burn, and I will kill you with the sword; *your wives will become widows and your children fatherless*" (emphasis added).

Also, the context of the psalm in its entirety answers the curse of Deuteronomy 27:19a: "Cursed be the one who perverts justice due the alien, the fatherless, and the widow."

Moreover, Psalm 109 recalls the promise of Yahweh to visit the iniquity of the fathers upon their children (Exod. 20:5–6; 34:7).[28] See Psalm 109:14, "May the iniquity of his fathers be remembered before Yahweh," and related curses uttered in reference to the descendants of the offender. David is calling upon God to act as he had promised—in literal, if horrid, detail. As H. G. L. Peels observes, such imprecatory prayers are heard from within the context of the covenant relationship between God and his people:

> The covenant is threatened by the fury of the godless. It is not they who are being killed but the righteous, and nobody intervenes. When in this situation the psalmist raises an imprecatory prayer to God and pleads for the punishment of the enemy, he ties in with God's own covenant curse upon the godless.[29]

Continuing Promise

The question again may be asked, *Is this covenant promise of divine cursing relevant to Christians?* In answer, the New Testament affirms the enduring validity of the Abrahamic promise for all who embrace Christ through faith: "If you belong to Christ, then you belong to Abraham's seed—heirs according to the promise" (Gal. 3:29). If, then, one is heir to the Abrahamic covenant, one is heir to the promise of blessing and cursing.[30] This dual-edged promise, finding its echo in the New Testament era, was not merely a spiritual abstraction. In discrete instances, it applied as well to the corporeal life of God's people in their times of extremity.

When, for example, Jesus sent out the Twelve, he instructed them that if they were welcomed into a home, they were to let their peace remain on it. That is, God, through his disciples, would bless those who blessed them. But if they were refused a welcome, they were to shake the dust off their feet as a sign of peace's antithesis—the curse of coming judgment. That is, God, through his disciples, would curse those who cursed them (Matt. 10:11–15). [31] This action, though voiceless, was an implicit imprecation.[32]

This same covenant principle is reinforced by Christ's own teaching in Luke 18:1–8. Jesus gives, as consolation for his own covenant "elect" in their settings of desperation (v. 7), the example of a widow pleading for vengeance against her adversary (v. 3). This continuing application of the Abrahamic curse in the life of the believer is further illustrated by the apostle Paul when he assured his protégé Timothy that a certain Alexander, who "cursed" God's people by strongly opposing both Paul and the gospel message, would in turn be cursed by God with divine retribution (2 Tim. 4:14–15). Although toned down from imprecation to assurance, Paul's solemn assertion still echoes the spirit of Psalm 109.[33]

Psalm 109 is a harsh and explicit appeal to the Lord of the covenant to remain true to his promise to curse those who curse his people. The promise commenced with Abraham (Gen. 12:3) and remains tacitly intact (e.g., Gal. 3:5–9, 16–18). In its canonical function in the community of faith, this psalm is the cry of the child of God who has no other recourse for justice. No other aid is available for the redress of grievous personal wrongs. The abuses of one's enemies have reached the extent that the honor and goodness of God are in question. The name of God and the enduring faith of his people are at stake.

It is from such a context that this prayer was first offered. In such a context, it may be appropriate still.

There is both personal and intercessory application of this psalm in the community of faith. In particular, it applies to victims of violent crime. Walter Brueggemann reflects that the cry of this psalm could be, for example, "the voice of a woman who is victimized by rape, who surely knows the kind of rage and indignation and does not need 'due process' to know the proper outcome. . . . For such as these, the rage must be carried to heaven, because there is no other court of appeal. 'Love of neighbor' surely means to go to court with the neighbor who is grieved."[34] And Erich Zenger observes that prayer such as this "can help the *victims* of violence, by placing on their lips a cry for justice and for the God of vengeance, to hold fast to their human dignity and to endure *nonviolently,* in prayerful protest against a violence that is repugnant to God, despite their fear in the face of their enemies."[35]

Part 3

Colliding with the
New Testament

Six

Apparent Contradictions

The Enemy, My Neighbor

"Love Your Enemies"

As arranged in Matthew's gospel, the Sermon on the Mount (Matt. 5–7) is presented as the grounding expression of Christian ethics.[1] Arising from its midst, and arriving at the climax of Christ's discourse on the Law in Matthew 5:17–48, comes the startling cry, "Love your enemies" (v. 44a). This portion of his oration is replete with radical statements that appear to contradict the teaching of the Old Testament.

This contradiction is more apparent, however, than real. Jesus himself introduces his several internalized and intensified "re-statements" of the Old Testament with the words, "Do not think that I have come to abolish the Law or the Prophets; I have not come to abolish, but to fulfill" (Matt. 5:17). In these words Jesus certified that he did not come to set himself up as a rival to the Old Testament. He does not disparage nor discredit what has come before. Rather, the Old Testament propels us *toward* Christ, it is summed up *in* Christ, and it must be interpreted *through* Christ.[2] D. A. Carson agrees that "Jesus does not conceive of his life and ministry in terms of *opposition* to the Old Testament, but in terms of *bringing to fruition* that toward which it points. Thus, the Law and the Prophets, far from being abolished, find their valid continuity in terms of their out-working in Jesus."[3]

In what follows (Matt. 5:21–48), Jesus affirms the Old Testament by reiterating—via hyperbole[4]—the original intent of several commands, contrary to the prevailing Pharisaical and scribal understanding of them. He plunged to the heart of the matter—the intent and implications of the commands, based upon his own authority. This was a radical move in itself, for Christ was placing himself on the level of the Lawgiver, God. The crowds recognized such authority. Indeed, the contrast between the authority of Christ and that of the Jewish religious leaders was publicly evident. At the conclusion of his sermon, the crowds were awed by the import and impact of his words (7:28–29).

Moreover, these restatements of Christ are framed by an inclusion of "impossible righteousness," both surpassing that of the Pharisees (5:20) and comparable to that of God (v. 48).[5] The climax of this teaching are his words in verses 43–45, 48:[6]

> [43]You have heard that it was said, "You shall love your neighbor and hate your enemy." [44]But I say to you, "Love your enemies and pray for those who persecute you, [45]so that you may be sons of your Father who is in heaven; for he causes his sun to rise on the evil and the good, and he sends rain on the righteous and the unrighteous. . . . [48]Be perfect, therefore, as your heavenly Father is perfect."[7]

The first half of Jesus' initial statement of the Pharisees' view in Matthew 5:43, "You shall love your neighbor," is a quotation from Leviticus 19:18. These words in Leviticus come directly after a prohibition of revenge or personal grudge. Jesus elsewhere testified that this tenet is the second-greatest commandment (Matt. 22:39; Mark 12:31; cf. Luke 10:27). The latter half of Jesus' quotation of the Pharisees, "You shall hate your enemy," is not found in the Old Testament.[8] Yet there is a likely connection between the mind-set behind this quotation and that of the Rule of the Qumran Community (1QS). This document begins with the resolve of the members "to love all the Sons of Light—each according to his lot in the counsel of God, and to hate all the Sons of Darkness—each according to his guilt at the vengeance of God" (1QS 1:9–11).[9] This hatred involved even the withholding of compassion (10:20–21).[10] It appears that many people of Jesus' day had come to believe that, if the Old Testament commanded the love of one's neighbor, it must also command hatred of one's enemy.[11] This understanding is expressed in the second century B.C. apocryphal Sirach 12:4–7:[12]

> [4]Give to the godly man, but do not help the sinner.
> [5]Do good to the humble, but do not give to the ungodly;
> hold back his bread, and do not give it to him,
>   lest by means of it he subdue you;
> for you will receive twice as much evil
>   for all the good which you do to him.
> [6]For the Most high also hates sinners
>   and will inflict punishment on the ungodly.
> [7]Give to the good man, but do not help the sinner.[13]

But Jesus says, "Love your enemies." He shocked his listeners by asserting the unthinkable: his followers are to "love" those whom they "hate" (or who hate them). Such love toward these people does not discount their remaining enemies. But, in a sense, the enemy becomes a neighbor. In the context of Christ's radical love command in Matthew 5:43–48, he defines *enemy* in such a way as to include both those who are foes in the political-national sense and those whose enmity is primarily interior. This includes enemies who are from among one's own people—that body of folk who are in Leviticus 19:18 explicitly considered one's neighbors. Indeed, this enmity of the heart is his point of emphasis.[14]

In this brief passage, *enemy* is placed parallel to *those who persecute you* (Matt. 5:44), "the evil" and "unrighteous" (v. 45), implicitly "those who do not love you" (v. 46), "tax collectors"—who were among their own people, but largely considered greedy and oppressive traitors (v. 46)— and implicitly "those who aren't your brothers" and "Gentiles" (v. 47).

Likewise, in the parable of the Good Samaritan (Luke 10:25–37),[15] Jesus expands the concept of *neighbor* beyond its initial meaning. In this parable Jesus drives home that the heart of the command, *Love your neighbor,* includes implicitly, *Love your enemy.* For to the question, *Who is my neighbor?* (v. 29), Jesus answers in essence, "Your enemy." This is true whether from the perspective of the Jew towards the Samaritan, or vice versa (cf. John 4:9); for he asks in response, "Who was the neighbor to this man?" (Luke 10:36). To Jesus, my "neighbor" may, indeed, be my "enemy." The one who is in need, and whose need I may meet, is my neighbor—whoever that may be.

In addition, the expression of kindness, as shown in this parable, is essentially love in action. And in the Sermons on the Mount and Plain, this love is patterned after the action of God, a God who freely exhibits kindness and compassion toward the evil and ungrateful (Luke 6:35–36), thus expressing his perfection (Matt. 5:48). And this love characterized by indiscriminate kindness toward friend and foe alike is a "perfection" his followers are to imitate.[16]

Implicit to Explicit

This enemy-love in deeds of kindness is not foreign to the Old Testament. Indeed, in certain instances, the Old Testament unquestionably commands kindness toward enemies. Exodus 23:4–5 says, for example, "If you happen upon the stray ox or donkey of your enemy, you must surely return it to him. If you see the donkey of one who hates you fallen under its load, do not fail to help him; you must surely help him with it."[17] Likewise, Proverbs 25:21–22 states, "If one who hates you is hungry, give him food to eat; and if he is thirsty, give him water to drink. For fiery coals you will heap on his head, and Yahweh will reward you."[18]

Saints of old obeyed this command. Of notable mention is Naaman's Israelite slave girl, who sought the welfare of her enemy master—the Aramean army commander. Yahweh responded kindly to him through his prophet Elisha (2 Kings 5).[19] Further, Elisha, in 2 Kings 6:18–23 counseled to feed rather than kill the enemy Arameans, who had been captured through a display of divine power. In this case, Elisha apparently reasoned that kindness at this point might ease the feelings of enmity. It seems to have done just that (v. 23b).

While it must be granted that the command to "love your enemies" is nowhere to be found in the Old Testament, the concept "cannot be confined to the words themselves. When enemies are fed and cared for, rather than killed or mistreated, love for enemy is being practiced."[20] Even in the context of Leviticus 19, *neighbor* is defined more broadly than its immediate parallel, *brother*. One's neighbor includes all within the community, including resident aliens.[21]

Leviticus 19 orders that both fellow Israelites and resident foreigners were to be loved "as yourself." Compare verse 18b, "And you shall love your neighbor as yourself," with verse 34b, "And you shall love him [i.e., the foreigner in your midst] as yourself." Although the term גֵּר (*gēr*) speaks generically of a "resident alien,"[22] in this context is the recognition of an implicit or provisional status of enmity as well.[23] Although Israel entered Egypt on friendly terms, their "sojourn" in Egypt was characterized by the enmity of slavery. It was this mistreatment of the Israelites by the Egyptians that Yahweh sought to counter among his own people, in opposition to their own inclinations to oppress and treat foreigners with suspicion.

Leviticus 19:33 confronts the natural reaction of mistreating such a foreigner.[24] Thus, a subtle sense of enmity, yet combined with the command of love—to be expressed in deeds of kindness—is indeed borne out in this passage.

Jesus, then, rather than presenting a novel idea or imposing a foreign interpretation on Leviticus 19, was in this regard both distilling and radicalizing the essence of the Old Testament teaching. In his terse command, however, he distinctly moves beyond the oblique teaching of the Old Testament and its case law. Now the demand for enemy-love is overt. Emphasis rests on what would have been considered the generally "unthinkable," as far as characteristic attitude and action are concerned.

Enemy-love and Curse

Arriving at these words of Jesus after having passed through the imprecatory psalms, however, raises the usual difficult question: In commanding his followers to "love their enemies," was Jesus utterly displacing the barbaric pleas exclaimed in these psalms? Certainly in extreme circumstances, Jesus did not hesitate to pronounce imprecation (e.g., Mark 11:12–14, 20–21), and he uttered excoriating woes against hardened unbelief (e.g., Matt. 11:20–24; 23:13–39). Now, although woes may be generally distinguished from curses, they are closely related. They bear a large measure of similarity and partial semantic overlap.[25]

This does not mean that Jesus acted out of accord with his own radi-cal dictum.[26] By Christ's own witness and example, this enemy-love is the attitude of readiness to show sustained and indiscriminate kindness. If, however, the enemy's cup of iniquity has become full to overflowing, this love is overtaken by the demands of justice and divine vengeance. Jesus' approach in this regard is strikingly similar to that of the psalmists who penned harsh words. David, for example, by his testimony in Psalms 35:11–17 and 109:4–5, demonstrated habitual kindness toward enemies, only to receive abuse in return. His was an example of extreme love—and a love that finally and fittingly met its extremity.[27]

In the broader view, then, rather than being completely incompatible, *enemy-love* and *enemy-curse* are found, strangely, to complement one another.[28]

Quick to Bless, Slow to Curse

"Bless and Curse Not"

Paul speaks to this complementary state from within that "masterful summary of Christian ethics"[29] (Rom. 12:9–21). His words are reminis-cent of Christ's words to "bless those who curse you" (Luke 6:28a) and "pray for those who persecute you" (Matt. 5:44b; cf. Luke 6:28b).[30] Paul's exhortation is, "Bless[31] those who persecute you; bless and do not curse" (Rom. 12:14). Herein lies one of the most difficult statements of Scrip-ture, one that runs counter to the Christian, indeed, the human consti-tution. For when evil people persecute, the instinct is to curse, yet the Christian is enjoined to bless.

Romans 12:9–21 is no haphazard collection of ethical injunctions. Its highly stylized structure presents teaching that is summed up in, and subsumed under, the introductory heading of "genuine love" (ἡ ἀγάπη ἀνυπόκριτος, *hē agapē anypokritos*). Genuine love is a love that, above all, abhors what is evil and adheres to what is good (v. 9). The verses that follow this heading explain what that sincere love looks like.

Moreover, the command to bless enemies is framed by the call both to "hate evil, clinging to the good" (v. 9) and to "conquer evil with good" (v. 21).[32]

David Alan Black observes that the overt repetition of these words "is a major device for defining Romans 12:9–21 as a literary unit. Not only does it signal the beginning and end of the unit, but it binds the intervening material together, suggesting that what is embraced within the brackets belongs together."[33] In some manner, then, the Christian is to wish the wicked well (see v. 14)[34] while hating the wickedness (v. 9b). Thus, in the right context and with proper motivation, holy hatred and genuine goodness join hands (vv. 19–20; cf. Ps. 35).

With the examples of genuine love sketched in this passage, the command to "bless" in Romans 12:14 receives special emphasis by its use of the imperative as opposed to the prevalence of participles. This emphasis is reinforced by the repetition of the command and the prohibition of its opposite: "Do not curse."

Paul's emphasis here demonstrates that love, the dominant Christian virtue, "reaches its climax in the love of enemies. Love is intended not only to permeate the relationship of Christians to one another but to shape their attitudes towards even those who seek their ruin."[35] Fundamental obedience to this unqualified command is revealed in a readiness to meet the physical needs of the enemy (Rom. 12:20) and a desire for the enemy's spiritual welfare. Love is shown in a desire that the enemy come to eternal life in Christ. This is the ultimate manifestation of blessing over cursing. The evil that undergirds this enmity, however, is no less abhorrent (v. 9), "for if there is no intense hatred (ἀποστυγοῦντες [*apostygountes*])[36] of evil, then there will be no intense love for one's enemy. Indeed, the good that love desires is primarily the removal of the cause of enmity, which is unbelief."[37]

How is the believer able to hate evil yet love the enemy? The admonitions "Repay no one evil for evil" (Rom. 12:17) and "Do not avenge yourselves" (v. 19) do not allow the Christian to mete out personal retribution. The Christian can be assured, however, of God's just revenge, now or in the coming Judgment (vv. 19–20). Although not stated here, the understanding elsewhere in Scripture is that the believer may call on him to do so at appropriate times.[38] In the climax of the parable of the unjust judge (Luke 18:7–8), for example, Jesus assured his disciples that God will indeed exact vengeance in response to the cries of his people—ostensibly, their cries for vengeance (cf. v. 3). Likewise, in Romans 12:9–21, the foundation upon which these ethical injunctions are laid is the confidence of divine justice. Paul bases his remarks on the promise of God in Deuter-onomy 32:35—"Vengeance is mine; I will repay"—and on the certainty expressed in Proverbs 25:21–22—kindness spurned will not go unan-swered by the divine Avenger (Rom. 12:19–20).

Enemy Blessing and Curse

How does one relate this dictum of Paul to the vehement curses of, for example, Psalm 109?[39] In Romans 12, Paul is speaking in terms of prin-ciple, that is, of the general characteristics and sentiments of a true Chris-tian—in much the same way that Jesus speaks in the Sermon on the Mount. The imprecatory psalms, though, as do the other imprecatory passages of both Old and New Testaments, arise out of extreme circum-stances—circumstances that warrant the appeal to extreme ethics. Mar-tin Luther admits the possibility of such circumstances, in which "it is wrong not to curse."[40] The resolution can be found in the phrase "be quick to bless and slow to curse"—a mind-set well expressed by E. W. Hengstenberg:

> Just as Christ did not at first come to condemn the world, but that the world through him might be saved, so also with the Christian, when he sees enmity against God's word, his king-dom or his servants, the first movement of his soul should be to pray to God that he would soften these hard hearts and open these blind eyes—a movement to which the Psalmists also were not strangers.[41]

This concept of "quick to bless and slow to curse" finds its pattern ech-oed in the divine and Christian character trait, "slow to anger." In Eph-esians 4:31 and Colossians 3:8, anger (ὀργη, *orgē*) is considered sin. Yet, in both Testaments, the Lord is displayed as expressing anger—and in graphic terms (e.g., Nah. 1:2; Mark 3:5); thus, anger cannot be deemed inherently sinful without impugning the character of God. Yahweh resolves this ap-parent paradox in his self-description as "slow to anger" (Exod. 34:6; cf. Nah. 1:3). This is translated into the Christian life as "let every man be quick to hear, slow to speak, slow to anger" (James 1:19).[42]

Seven

Heaping Coals of Fire

Terrorist attacks in the United States on September 11, 2001, confronted humanity with a glaring reality: seething enmity exists, and it will erupt in targeted violence. And in recent years, Christians have been reawakened to the unrelenting scourge of violence against their brothers and sisters around the world. Followers of Christ do suffer imprisonment and beatings. Their property is destroyed. They are targets of economic and societal discrimination. They are sold into slavery, cruelly raped, unjustly executed, and frivolously murdered. The sole reason for these horrors is that they bear the name of Christ. In the face of such true evil, what should the Christian response be?

Romans 12:17–21 addresses this very question. As noted above, the larger passage, beginning in verse 9, is a premier section in Paul's thought, unified under the heading of "genuine love." Verses 9–21 unwrap what that real love looks like in a series of concrete examples. At its climax, the text arrives at the hardest test. Real love affects how a person relates to those who hate him or her. Love marks Christians (John 13:35), and what sets Christians apart is that they love even their enemies.

But how are Christians to show "real love" to an enemy? What does this love look like, and how is the Christian able to sustain it? Romans 12:17–21 includes the following admonition, which draws on Deuteronomy 32:35 and Proverbs 25:21–22:

[17]Do not repay anyone evil for evil. .... [19]Do not avenge your-selves, beloved; but give place to (God's) wrath, for it is written:

> "Vengeance is mine, I will repay," says the Lord;
> [20]but "If your enemy is hungry, feed him;
> if he is thirsty, give him (something) to drink;
>   for in doing this you will heap coals of fire upon his head."

[21]Do not be conquered by evil, but conquer evil with good.

The Meaning of the Image

The question of how to show love to enemies is dominated in Romans 12 by the image of "coals of fire" (v. 20b)—an image that has ignited and sustained a furor of debate across the centuries. The language of Proverbs embedded in Paul's quotation is evocative. Proverbs 25:21–22 states,

> [21]If one who hates you is hungry, give him food to eat;
>   and if he is thirsty, give him water to drink.
> [22]For you will heap fiery coals on his head,
>   and Yahweh will reward you.

What is the meaning of these "coals of fire," and what impact does it have on the Christian ethic of enemy-love? Three interpretations have dominated the debate over this passage through church history, two of which trace their lineage back to at least the fourth century. "Coals of fire" has been argued to represent (1) a symbol of shame, (2) a picture of repentance, or (3) an image of divine justice.

The first position, advanced by Augustine (354–430), holds that "coals of fire" refers to the burning pangs of shame that the enemy will experience upon being shown such kindness. The acts may lead to repentance and reconciliation. This view finds some warrant in the ancient Egyptian *Instruction of Amen-Em-Opet* (chap. 2), which similarly advocates "feeding" an enemy so that he might feel "ashamed."

> Thou heated man, how art thou [now]?
> He is crying out, and his voice [reaches] to heaven.
> O moon, establish his crime [against him]!
> So steer that we may bring the wicked man across,
> For we shall not act like him—
> Lift him up, give him thy hand;
> Leave him [in] the arms of the god;
> Fill his belly with bread of thine,
> So that he may be sated and may *be ashamed*.[1]

Such a meaning, however, runs counter to the way this image is used throughout the Old Testament.

The second position agrees with the first that the "coals of fire" is a positive image—but one that is not to be understood as a sense of shame. Rather the idea harks back to an actual Egyptian ritual of repentance, known from the demotic *Tale of Khamuas*. In this narrative, the bringing of "a forked stick in the hand and a censer of fire on the head"[2] tangibly demonstrated repentance to the party wronged. It is significant to note that in the tale itself, the repentance is more forced than heartfelt. Siegfried Morenz first drew the connection from "coals of fire," which appear in this tale, to the references in Proverbs and Romans.

The comparison is called into question on two accounts: (1) There is no mention of the "forked stick" in Proverbs 25:22, which is the alleged parallel to the tale. In that tale the two elements are inextricable. Moreover, this proverb refers to "coals" in lieu of Khamuas' "censer"— a distinction of significance if direct borrowing is to be construed. (2) The composition of Khamuas dates to the middle Ptolemaic times— roughly 233/232 B.C.[3] Although "the repentance ritual may antedate the literary document,"[4] it is far from certain that it does so by the seven centuries necessary to place it in the context of Solomon (cf. Prov. 25:1[5]). This view sees too much in Egypt and not enough in the Old Testament.

The third position was argued by John Chrysostom (347–407), who held that "coals of fire" refers to some future divine punishment awaiting those who spurn the Christian's deeds of love. If the enemy does not finally repent at such grace extended, he summons upon himself the sure judgment of God.[6] This tacit qualification is important, for God's forgiveness is always granted to the truly repentant.

Three pieces of evidence support this position that "coals of fire" represents divine judgment and that Romans 12:20 reinforces the message of verse 19: (1) the development of the imagery from the Old Testament; (2) the grammatical structure of these verses in their apparent parallelism; (3) the context in which they are located.

First, in the Old Testament, the imagery of "coals of fire" is invariably a symbol of divine anger and judgment. Most pertinent is Psalm 140:9–10:

> [10]The heads of those who surround me—
>   may he cover them with the trouble of their lips.
> [11]May fiery coals fall upon them;
>   may he throw them into the fire,
>   into watery pits—may they never rise!

Moreover, in Psalm 18, David describes God's indignant response and rescue of him from his enemies by, in part, this vivid description of "coals of fire" (v. 12). And Psalm 11:6 similarly promises, "He will rain on the wicked coals of fire and sulfur."[7] It seems unlikely that the apostle Paul would use such a potent image in a manner foreign to its common usage. Nothing in the context indicates that he is pouring new meaning into an old metaphor.[8]

Second, scrutiny of the structure of Romans 12:19–20 reveals a certain symmetry that suggests that the message of verse 20 should be construed as complementing and essentially restating verse 19. The primary command, "do not avenge yourselves, beloved," is counterweighted by two responses—one passive and one active: "*but* (ἀλλά, *alla*) give place to (God's) wrath" and "*but* (ἀλλά, *alla*) 'if your enemy is hungry, feed him; if he is thirsty, give him [something] to drink.'" What the one expresses in a passive sense with regard to the renunciation of personal vengeance, the other expresses in an active manner with regard to the doing of good.[9] In some measure, these deeds of kindness are compared to making room for God's wrath.

Third, the immediate context argues for such an understanding. Indeed, the principle of Christian non-retaliation enjoined by Paul in Romans 12:19 is explicitly based upon "deference to God's impending vengeance."[10] The issue Paul addresses is "how to act when all attempts to avoid conflict with the enemies of God and of his Church have failed"[11] (vv. 17–18). In such circumstances, the Christian is to continue to respond in love, entrusting justice to the God who has promised to repay the impenitent.

In this way, these verses are similar to what Paul had earlier addressed in Romans 2:4–5:

> Or do you show contempt for the riches of his kindness and forbearance and long-suffering, not knowing that the kindness of God leads you to repentance? But because of your stubbornness and unrepentant heart, you are storing up for yourself wrath in the day of wrath and revelation of the righteous judgment of God.

God's kindness is to lead to repentance, but persistence in unrepentance has the promise of wrath.

Thus, implicit in the affirmation that the Lord will repay (Rom. 12:19), heaping coals of fire on the head of the enemy (v. 20), is the condition of continued enmity, that is, *if* the enemy remains hostile.[12] Divine grace is ever extended to the repentant. Within the larger context of verses 9–21, verses 19–20 function not only to reemphasize the grounding ethic and characteristic activity of the Christian; the text also consoles the believer in the face of stubborn enmity and explains that a just God is at work, even when only injustice can be seen. Christians are indeed called to seek the benefit of those who hate them (v. 14), but grace repeatedly spurned holds the assurance of divine vengeance (v. 19).

Non-retaliation and "Retaliation"

But if "heaping coals of fire" is an image of looming divine vengeance, doesn't this strike against the core ethical principle of love and bring into doubt the purity of the person's motivation? It sounds much like the caricature idea: "Do good to your enemy so that his punishment will be all the more severe."[13] No, in the relevant context, it is rather a positive word of comfort for the Christian in the face of stubborn and unrepentant enmity. God's judgment is by no means the *motivation* for deeds of love, but judgment does lay the *foundation* upon which the altar of radical love is raised. Christians have the freedom to radically love under the assurance of divine vengeance.[14]

The natural human response to injustice is to lash out, to return the same measure of damage that was inflicted by the evil. Thus the opening to this section speaks the warning, "Do not repay anyone evil for evil" (Rom. 12:17). Then the thought is fleshed out to give a fuller understanding of the text: "Give place to [God's] wrath" (v. 19). The passive element of Paul's argument may be rephrased as "Don't retaliate—but relinquish to God." The wronged person must relinquish the "rights" of retaliation to the wrath of God, knowing that in the end he will make everything "right."[15] This "blessed assurance" of God's ultimate justice frees from any concern about the demands of interpersonal injustices.[16] It allows expressions of radical love. As the second greatest commandment itself is framed: "Do not take revenge . . . but love your neighbor as yourself" (Lev. 19:18).

Romans 12:20 depicts the enemy in need. Now comes the tangible decision of the heart. Will action or instinct govern the person? Given human need, which will conquer—evil or good? (v. 21). The human instinct is to withhold assistance or to gloat over misfortune. But to "repay evil with evil" means that evil conquers. The only way to "conquer evil" is to answer evil with kindness. What that looks like in this passage is feeding in hunger, giving water in thirst. This is a very real demonstration of love. Thus, the active element of Paul's argument may be rephrased, "Do 'retaliate'—with radical acts of kindness."

We have been confronted with a recent example of this issue on a colossal scale. On December 26, 2004, and without warning, a massive tsunami wracked the coasts and islands of the north Indian Ocean, leaving an astronomical death toll in its wake (above 200,000). The regions hardest hit are some of the most active oppressors of God's people. Persecution of Christians is particularly pronounced in Indonesia, near the epicenter of the earthquake that started this wave of destruction. And yet, in a response befitting Paul's directive in verse 20, relief from Christians around the world rushed in.

Both facets of response to enmity appear in the life and teaching of Christ. First Peter 2:23 relates that "when he was reviled, he did not revile in return . . . but entrusted himself to the one who judges justly." And in his Sermon on the Plain, Jesus' astounding command to "love your enemies, do good to those who hate you, bless those who curse you, pray for those who mistreat you" (Luke 6:27–28ff.) is directly preceded by both the blessings and *woes* of God's final and just judgment (vv. 20–26). This is the background and basis on which Christ's people are called to counter instinct by extending tangible kindness to those who hate them.

The foundation for Jesus' radical command of enemy-love in the present is the assurance of God's righteous judgment in the future.[17] That is sure and that is *then*.

But *now* is the time to love. *Now* is the moment of mercy. This answers the initial question, *How are Christians to show "real love" to an enemy?* Love is demonstrated when wrath is left to God and kindness is shown in response to the enemy's need. Christians can *love all* so radically and indiscriminately because justice will be covered by the judgment of God. The assurance of God's ultimate justice (then) frees radical love (now).

After encountering the curses and pleas for divine vengeance in the imprecatory psalms, the Christian is at first taken aback by the startling demands of Christ and his apostles, injunctions that initially appear to counter and even overthrow the ethics of the prior age.

But in keeping with the progress of revelation, both the command of enemy-love and its ramifications are made more explicit and given greater emphasis. Further, the expectation of divine vengeance finds an increased eschatological focus.

In addition, although occurring with less frequency—and often with less vividness—the New Testament contains the conspicuous presence of extreme and even personalized curses, which remarkably bear no hint of condemnation.

To these New Testament curses the next chapter now turns.

Eight

New Testament Curses

Christ's staggering command to "love your enemies" and Paul's un-qualified "bless, and curse not" give in explicit form the characteristic ethic of the new era—the age of "grace upon grace," inaugurated in the coming of Christ. In these radical demands is evidenced a distinct progression in the ethic of enemy-love. Nowhere in the Old Testament are such commands stated in such language, so the New Testament words superficially seem to supercede the sentiment expressed in the imprecatory psalms.

Although, in this new age, the demands of love have been brought to the fore, they are not, in fact, wholly new demands. The two "great commands" of both testaments remain the same. But what was embryonic in the Old Testament finds full expression in Christ. Indeed, the New Testament ethic of enemy-love and blessing is intensified, and the implications of that ethic are more extensively explored and applied.

Imprecations are also found in the New Testament, though they arise infrequently. New Testament imprecations have the same rationale as the imprecatory psalms. These instances provide understanding about when it is, for Christians, "the time to curse."

Jesus: Curse of Utter Desolation

An instance of actual imprecation from the lips of Jesus is recorded in Mark 11:14. The curse was uttered *en route* to the temple courts and against a fig tree that had the appearance of vitality but no fruit. As both the near context and the larger development of the gospel make clear, Jesus' cursing of the fig tree is a not-so-veiled imprecation against faithless and fruitless Israel—an Israel that had stubbornly rejected him.[1] This rejection would culminate in the crucifixion. Christ's curse would find its zenith in the desolation of A.D. 70 when Jerusalem fell to the Romans.[2]

This exhibit of an object lesson by Christ belongs in a series of incidents that follow his triumphal entry into Jerusalem. That day he was heralded by the people as the promised Davidic Messiah-king (Mark 11:1–11). This series of events culminates in his prophecy of the imminent destruction of the very temple complex he had so recently cleansed (13:1–2).

That the rejection curse was indirectly placed upon his people[3] is further clarified in the parable of the tenants, which follows it (Mark 12:1–12, esp. v. 9).[4] This parable echoes the language and imagery of Isaiah 5:1–7—a solemn parable of judgment against God's people Israel that is followed by a succession of woes.

The curse of Christ is pointed, marking the distinct end of one era and the beginning of another: "May no one any longer eat fruit from you—ever!" (Mark 11:14).[5] Immediately following his curse, Christ moves into the temple precincts where, of all places, "God ought to receive the purest form of worship."[6] Instead he finds the basest form of corruption: greed. When Christ and his disciples later return along the same road following Christ's purge of the temple, Peter takes notice of this same tree, and marvels at the demonstrable effect of Christ's curse: "Rabbi, look! The fig tree that you cursed [κατηράσω, *katerasō*]—it has withered!" (v. 21). William Lane observes the intentional crafting of this immediate context:

> In the Gospel of Mark Jesus' action in the Temple is firmly embedded within the fig tree incident. The a-b-a structure of Ch. 11:12–21 (fig tree-cleansing of the Temple-fig tree) serves to provide a mutual commentary on these two events. Just as the leaves of the tree concealed the fact that there was no fruit to enjoy, so the magnificence of the Temple and its ceremony conceals the fact that Israel has not brought forth the fruit of righteousness demanded by God. Both incidents have the character of a prophetic

sign, which warns of judgment to fall upon Israel for honoring God with their lips when their heart was far from him.[7]

The near context strongly intimates that this curse was not directed against the fig tree *as such*. The tree was cursed for the disciples' benefit that they might understand Christ's imprecation against unrepentant Israel.[8] It was a sign of divine visitation in judgment.[9] This judgment marked the true realization of that curse. Christ's intention is indicated by the deliberate arrangement of this account as a literary "frame" to the temple cleansing (Mark 11:12–21). It is a dramatic moment, marking the rejection of Christ by his people and the judgement of his people by Christ (vv. 14, 18). Thus, this curse puts an end to God's program as it had been administered historically through the nation Israel. As R. A. Cole remarks regarding the intent of Christ's action,

> Unless we realize that this was an acted parable of Israel, we shall be puzzled by all sorts of irrelevant questions. . . . Henceforth Israel was to be blasted and fruitless; and the physical judgment of A.D. 70 was but an outward token of this. . . . [A]nd immediately below the Marcan fig tree passage, in verses 15–19, there comes the acted parable of the cleansing of the Temple. God came to His Temple looking for fruit and found none; and so it was inevitable that the predictions of Mark xiii.1,2 be made. . . . Like tree, like temple, like nation; the parallel is exact.[10]

Far from being an arbitrary choice or happenstance, Christ's curse of the fig tree was intentional, drawing from a long history of imagery familiar to his people. Compare, initially, this account with Christ's parable, uttered earlier in his earthly ministry (Luke 13:6–9), about a man whose patience with an unfruitful fig tree has been nearly expended. In this parable, the unfruitful fig tree unquestionably represents unrepentant Israel and serves as an illustration of his urgent call for his people to repent (vv. 1–5). Furthermore, in the Old Testament, the fig tree was frequently associated with the nation Israel: when verdant and fruitful, it was a picture of peace, prosperity, and divine blessing (e.g., 1 Kings 4:25; Mic. 4:4; Joel 2:22); when ravaged and withered, it served as "a vivid emblem of God's active *punishment* of his people."[11] In Jeremiah 8:13, for example, Yahweh includes this imagery in his judgment oracle against his rebellious people:

> I will put an end to them entirely, declares Yahweh:
> There will be no grapes on the vine;
> and there will be no figs on the fig-tree;
> and their foliage will wither.
> What I have given to them will be taken from them.[12]

In certain passages, moreover, God's judgment against Israel's fig trees is juxtaposed with Israel's rabid idolatry and the perversion of God's worship (e.g., Hos. 2:11–13). Of particular note is Hosea 9:10–17, in which Yahweh speaks of Israel's beginnings as "early figs on the fig tree" (v. 10), but because of their gross iniquity Yahweh promises to "drive them out of my House" (i.e., "temple," v. 15). And they who are named "Ephraim" (i.e., "fruitfulness") are instead "withered" and "bear no fruit" (v. 16).[13]

Mark's readers, steeped in the Old Testament, would, then, have readily understood Christ's cursing of the barren fig tree as a judgment directed against the nation Israel—and especially against their religious center, the temple. Christ's visitation here is reminiscent of the prophecy of Malachi, in which Yahweh promised to send his "Messenger of the Covenant" to his temple, to cleanse his priests and people (Mal. 3:1–5)—a coming accompanied by the threat of divine curse (חֵרֶם, *ḥērem*, 4:6). At his approach to the temple in its state of acute corruption and perversion and in light of the patent and repeated rejection of him by the leaders of his people, Christ parabolically expresses this curse.

Apostles: Spiritual and Physical Curses

Curse of Eternal Damnation

In addition to that of Christ, there are instances of apostolic imprecations.[14] In Galatians 1:8–9 (cf. 1 Cor. 16:22[15]), the apostle Paul utters what is unquestionably a curse of the severest magnitude—that of eternal damnation.

[8]But even if we or an angel from heaven should preach a gospel to you other than what we preached to you, let him be accursed! [9]As we have said before, so now I say again: If anyone should preach a gospel to you other than what you received, let him be accursed!

Transliterated, the term here rendered "accursed" is "anathema" (ἀνάθεμα). In Hellenistic Greek, this label was used to denote both "something dedicated or consecrated to the deity" as well as "something delivered up to divine wrath, dedicated to destruction and brought under a curse."[16] It was used in the Septuagint to translate the Hebrew חֵרֶם (ḥērem)[17]—a term characteristic of the Israelite "holy wars." Whatever was so designated was dedicated to Yahweh for total destruction. The Pauline usage of the term, likewise, refers to being brought under the divine curse—but here the curse of eternal condemnation. This connotation is confirmed by Romans 9:3, where Paul startles his readers by expressing the desire to become "accursed . . . from Christ" (emphasis added) if that would mean the salvation of his people. The villainy enacted by those who are the intended recipients[18] of Paul's imprecation is the perverting of the gospel of grace by enslaving it to the rigors of legalism. Those who seek to undermine the ground and sustenance of salvation truly merit the harshest of denunciations (cf. Jude 11–13; 2 Peter 2:14). The name of Christ is at stake.

Additionally, the apostle Peter—in confronting Simon the Sorcerer, who sought to purchase from him the power of the Holy Spirit—uttered the caustic curse, "May your money perish with you!" (Acts 8:20a). Such a scathing curse consigns Simon—and his money with him—to destruction (εἰς ἀπώλειαν, eis apōleian). It further functions as a solemn warning regarding what will surely happen to him if he does not change his attitude.[19]

However severe, this apostolic curse was to be actualized only if there was continued sin and impenitence. Such is shown by the exchange that directly follows, in which Peter voices a plea of repentance along with the offer of release: "Repent, then, of this evil of yours and pray to the Lord. Perhaps he will forgive you the intent of your heart" (Acts 8:22). Even in the midst of such imprecation there is ever implicit or explicit the hope of repentance and restoration.

Thus is gained additional insight into the maledictions of psalmist and apostle alike: "for all their appearance of implacability," writes Derek Kidner, "they are to be taken as conditional, as indeed the prophets' oracles were. . . . Their full force was for the obdurate; upon repentance they would become 'a curse that is causeless', which, as Proverbs 26:2 assures us, 'does not alight.'"[20]

Bodily Curses

In Acts 13:10–11b, Paul voices severe words against a certain Elymas the Sorcerer, attendant to the Roman proconsul of Cyprus, where Paul and Barnabas were ministering the gospel:

> [10]You son of the Devil! Enemy of all that is right! Full of all deceit and trickery! Will you never stop perverting the right ways of the Lord? [11]So now, behold! The hand of the Lord is against you, and you will be blind, unable to see the sun for some time!

When Sergius Paulus wished to hear the word of God from the apostles, Elymas raised strong opposition and sought to keep the proconsul from the faith. Only at this point does Paul act decisively, uttering an imprecation of blindness against him.[21] The imprecation is strikingly similar to the curses of both the Old Testament and other records from the ancient Near East.[22] Although this magician's name literally means "son of Jesus" ("Bar-Jesus," v. 6), Paul addresses him as "son of the Devil" (v. 10a), in accord with his work and character.

In addition, it is of import to note that this curse was uttered in keeping with the principle embodied in the *lex talionis:* since Elymas had sought to keep the proconsul in spiritual blindness, the magician was cursed with physical blindness.[23]

But is this example of Paul to serve as an example for us? John Calvin contends that it does: "Thus must we deal with the desperate enemies of the gospel, in whom appeareth open contumacy and wicked contempt of God, especially when they stop the way before others. And lest any man should think that Paul was out of measure angry, Luke saith plainly that the inspiration of the Spirit was his guide."[24] Indeed, Luke emphasizes that Paul was "filled with the Holy Spirit" (Acts 13:9) as he voiced his cry, leaving no doubt that his readers should regard Paul's act as right and proper in this context.

In his impassioned letter to the Galatian church, Paul utters execration at a more explicitly "physical" level against those who sought to enforce upon converts of Galatia certain demands, in particular physical circumcision, as a ritual necessary for salvation. This time he does so in graphic—even grotesque—words: "I wish even that those who are agitating you would emasculate themselves!" (Gal. 5:12). Such seemingly unbridled language is indeed troubling to our ears. William Klassen, for example, concludes that Paul commits a sin in this text, adding, "It can be understood and forgiven. Under no circumstances should it be made a model for Christian behavior."[25]

John Calvin counters, however, with an appropriate and pastoral response:

> Paul cannot be accused of cruelty, as if he were opposed to the law of love. . . . It is a cruel kind of mercy which prefers a single man to the whole church. "On one side, I see the flock of God in danger; on the other, I see a wolf 'seeking,' like Satan, 'whom he may devour.' (1 Pet. v. 8.) Ought not my care of the church to swallow up all my thoughts, and lead me to desire that its salvation should be purchased by the destruction of the wolf? And yet I would not wish that a single individual should perish in this way; but my love of the church and my anxiety about her interests carry me away into a sort of ecstasy, so that I can think of nothing else." With such a zeal as this, every true pastor of the church will burn.[26]

Martyrs in Heaven: The Plea for Divine Vengeance

The cry of the martyred saints in Revelation 6:10 is manifestly an appeal to a higher, divine court. Joel Musvosvi observes that the appeal is made "in the face of a gross miscarriage of justice that resulted in their [the martyrs] condemnation and death."[27] The martyrs demand promised justice: "How long, O Master, holy and true, until you judge the inhabitants of the earth and avenge our blood?"[28] This language bluntly harks back to the divine promise in the Song of Moses to "avenge the blood of his servants" (Deut. 32:43a). Such pleas are the backbone of the imprecatory psalms.

Notice in the following examples the coupling of the cry of divine vengeance with the call "How long?":

> [5]How long, O Yahweh, will you be angry forever;
>   Will your jealousy burn like fire?
> [6]Pour out your wrath upon the nations
>   that do not know you. . . .
> [10]. . . Before our eyes, make known among the nations
>   that you avenge the outpoured blood of your servants.
>   —Psalm 79:5–6, 10

> [1]God of vengeance, O Yahweh,
>   God of vengeance, shine forth!
> [2]Rise up, Judge of the earth;
>   Pay back to the proud what they deserve!
> [3]How long will the wicked, O Yahweh,
>   How long will the wicked exult?[29]
>   —Psalm 94:1–3

Further, the development of the book of Revelation is largely a divine response to the martyrs' cry. Revelation 16:5–6, for instance, in response to the realization of God's judgments, issues the praise, "You are just . . . for they have shed the blood of saints and prophets." Revelation 18:20, 24 similarly rings out, "Rejoice! . . . for God has judged her for the way she treated you. . . . In her was found the blood of prophets and saints." Notice particularly, at the climax of the Apocalypse, the cry of the heavenly crowd: "Hallelujah! . . . He has avenged the blood of his servants" (19:1b–2).

It is significant that the condition of these martyred saints in having moved on to their heavenly abode "guarantees," notes Robert L. Thomas, "the absence of any selfish motives in their prayer life."[30] What is striking about their petition, however, is the consequent justification of like prayers uttered by saints on earth. If it is praiseworthy for perfected saints to pray thus, then it is presumably so for those who inhabit this fallen earth.[31] Moreover, the Song of Moses (Deut. 32), which provides the foundation for the theology of divine vengeance and to which the martyrs' appeal is implicitly connected, is mentioned in Revelation 15:3.[32] There, at the close of the ages, the saints in heaven are found celebrating the Song's promised actualization in the judgments of Christ by singing "the Song of Moses the servant of God and the Song of the Lamb."

Although few in number, noteworthy examples can nonetheless be found from the New Testament, citing "the time to curse." Instructive is Christ's own curse of the fig tree as an illustration against the nation of Israel. The nation's religious leadership had long been full of iniquity, and all the people would bear the consequences, a judgment realized in the destruction of Jerusalem and its temple.

The apostles Peter and Paul were known to utter the curse of eternal damnation on those who sought to pervert or otherwise undermine the gospel of grace. Paul did not shirk from pronouncing physical curses as well.

The perfected martyrs in heaven, out of their unanswered desolation, likewise call out to God for the avenging of their blood, using language starkly similar to certain imprecations in the psalms.

As with the Old Testament imprecations, the curses of the New Testament are uttered against the stubbornly rebellious as well as those dangerous to the faith or violent against the faithful. Such utterances are, according to the presentations of the texts themselves, entirely justified. It is perhaps surprising that, in some fashion, the cry of imprecation and the appeal to God for vengeance comports with the ethic of enemy-love and blessing as expressed in both the Old and New Testaments.

Conclusion

This present work has argued and defended the premise that the imprecatory psalms[1] retain an appropriate place in the life of the Christian church. *It is legitimate at times for God's present people to utter prayers of imprecation or pleas for divine vengeance—like those in the psalms— against the recalcitrant enemies of God and his people. Such expression is consistent with the ethics of the Old Testament and finds corresponding echo in the New.*

This position is rooted, first, in the establishment of the psalms' theology of imprecation as the very essence of Torah. The principles of such theology were well established in the promise of divine vengeance expressed in the Song of Moses, the principle of divine justice outlined in the *lex talionis*, and the assurance of divine cursing as well as blessing articulated in the inaugural covenant of God with his people. Second, this theology continues essentially unchanged through to the end of the canon and is used to undergird the imprecations in the New Testament, infrequent though they are.

Moreover, in addressing this issue of imprecations in the psalms, certain factors were initially noted.

First, the vengeance appealed for by the pious in the imprecatory psalms was never personally enacted. Rather the appeal was always explicitly or implicitly addressed to God. The realization of that vengeance was left to him alone.

Second, the characteristically impassioned imprecatory pleas were based on the covenant promises of God. The most notable of these promises is "he who curses you, I will curse" (Gen. 12:3), and "vengeance is mine, I will repay" (Deut. 32:35).

Third, both testaments record examples of God's people on earth calling down curses or crying for vengeance, the expression of neither sentiment accompanied by any textual hint of divine disapproval. Rather, in their limited and appropriate circumstance, such utterances are presented as justified and commendable. Indeed, Scripture records an instance in which God's perfected saints in heaven appeal for divine vengeance, using language reminiscent of certain of the imprecatory psalms. They are comforted by the assurance that judgment is near (Rev. 6:9–11).

It is important to recognize the contexts out of which such imprecations were uttered (from the psalms through apostolic era), for they were invariably of an extreme nature. Any imprecation in the psalms comes only after the enemy has repeatedly returned evil for good, or after gross, vicious, or sustained injustice. The objects of the psalmists' imprecations have characteristically abused power, oppressed the helpless, and committed unthinkable and unpunished acts of evil. Out of such circumstances, the plea of the righteous arises for the God of the covenant and the God of justice to make himself known.

It was observed that the essential morality prescribed in Scripture has remained constant, as shown in the testimony of Christ himself. This overarching divine demand and characteristic ethic of God's people—based on the character and activity of God—is love, an unreserved love of God and of one's neighbor. The implications latent in this latter command, in particular, however, are unwrapped and even intensified in the early teachings of Christ. "Love your neighbor" becomes also "Love your enemies."

This expansion of enemy-love is tied to the era of fulfillment and the transition of God's people from a centralized to a decentralized entity. In the Old Testament, God's people were surrounded by enemy nations. The necessity of their survival and the fulfillment of God's promises required a prevailing posture of caution. But with the coming of Christ as the culmination of the ages, as well as the outpouring of the Spirit as the climax of promise, has come a more explicit embrace of enemy-love and enduring abuse, coupled with the opening of the nations to the gospel of grace.

In this difference of circumstances is the ready recognition of a degree of difference, too, in emphasis between the testaments. In the New Testament, less stress is placed on imprecation and the enactment of temporal judgments. This is combined with more frequent and explicit calls for kindness in anticipation of the eschatological judgment. Also, there is a more overt identification of fundamental enmities at the spiritual level.

But this difference in the progress of the testaments is a difference in degree, rather than a difference in kind. In principle, "loving" and "blessing" is the dominant mood of the New Testament, as it is of the Old Testament, albeit in a more subdued fashion. The imprecatory passages of both Old Testament and New Testament, however, supplement this general tone. They articulate the minor—yet complementary—ethic demonstrated in instances of extremity. Indeed, the New Testament still finds a legitimate place for imprecation, based on the same elements as serve to justify the imprecations in the Psalms. Thus, enemy-love and enemy-imprecation are harmonizable tensions found through both testaments and must be properly dealt with by God's people in whatever dispensation they appear.

The introduction of this current work broached as its subject the imprecatory psalms with respect to Christian ethics: *What is the reconciliation between the graphic and prolific curses against enemies in the psalms and the Christian calls to "love your enemies" and to "bless, and curse not"?* The question is all the more relevant given an increased awareness of vicious hostility directed against Christians by those with other worldviews. But there is an initial stigma attached to the concept of divine vengeance. This stigma, however, is somewhat assuaged when one understands that the vengeance of God on his enemies is the necessary obverse of the deliverance of his people from their enemies.

Chapter 1 investigated the principal solutions proposed to explain the relation of the Christian to these psalms, and their legitimacy was evaluated in light of the Scriptures of both testaments. The imprecatory psalms have been chiefly explained by one of the following:

1. *They are expressions of evil emotions, either to be utterly avoided or expressed to God and relinquished there.* This position fails to

adequately account for the imprecatory psalms being inspired by God and the profusion of imprecations in the psalms, which were incorporated in the canon. It also does not sufficiently address the piety of the psalmists and their ethical rationale, the legitimacy of their utterance in light of their Old Testament theological foundations, and the presence of similar imprecations in the New Testament.

2. *They were in keeping with the moral character of the old covenant but are inconsistent with the ethos of the new era.* This position, however, overly restricts the definition of love and minimizes the fundamental ethical continuity between the testaments in the outworking of progressive revelation. It does not sufficiently account for the enduring validity of the Abrahamic promise or the presence of personalized imprecations in the New Testament.

3. *They are words appropriately uttered solely from the lips of Christ in relation to his work on the cross, and consequently only by his followers through him.* This position, however, overstates David's position and function as a type of Christ, understates the reality of the historical situations that evoke the utterances, and evades the problem that David did not write all of the imprecatory psalms, let alone the other imprecations in Scripture.

These views being found unsatisfactory for their varying reasons, create the need for a satisfactory solution.

Chapter 2 sought to station the imprecatory psalms in their ancient Near Eastern context, in which cursing was a facet of everyday life. Curses were used in treaties and can be read in numerous burial inscriptions and incantations. In addition, in the ancient Near East, the distinction was made between a legitimate curse and an illegitimate curse. A witch's incantation was an illegitimate curse, but it was legitimate to use curses in suzerain-vassal treaties and the psalms. Moreover, the fulfillment of the legitimate curse was ceded to the god under whose jurisdiction it lay or to whom appeal was made. Thus, for the faithful Israelite, the effect and fulfillment of an imprecation depended solely on the character and activity of God.

Part 2 of this study explored the three harshest psalms of imprecation.

Cries of cursing came out of extreme circumstances and a clear biblical and theological understanding. These three psalms in particular were chosen, not only because they represent the three spheres of cursing found in the Psalter, but also because they are the most vividly harsh and notorious of the imprecatory psalms. Thus, a satisfactory justification that is discovered for these will apply appropriately to all.

The cries of Psalm 58 arise out of a context of societal desperation. Those in positions of judicial authority have exploited their power for evil and their own ends. They chronically and violently flaunt their position, contrary to God's righteousness. Rather than protecting the helpless under their care, the authorities have instead persecuted and preyed upon them. The psalmist's imprecations evidently find their motivation in the promise of divine vengeance articulated in Deuteronomy 32, the Song of Moses. Elements of this poetic section of Torah, including the joy of the righteous at the realization of divine vengeance, are carried through the canon to the end of the New Testament (see Rev. 15:3; 18:20; 19:1–2).

Psalm 137 is sung from the context of the Babylonian exile—a religious and national calamity preceded by the unspeakable horrors and cruelties of ancient siege warfare. The primary basis for its appalling beatitudes is the principle of divine justice expressed in the *lex talionis*—a law not of private retaliation but of just recompense, indeed a law that serves as the basis for any civilized judicial system. This appeal for "talionic justice" likewise finds expression throughout the Scriptures, even to the end of the New Testament (e.g., 2 Tim. 4:14; Rev. 18:6).

The litany of curses seen in Psalm 109 arises out of a situation of desperate need. For his sustained love and goodness, David has been repaid with vicious hatred and grave evil. Thus, David makes appeal to the covenant promise of God—initially expressed in Genesis 12:3—with its assurance of divine cursing on those who would curse his people. And the Abrahamic promise remains tacitly intact into the New Testament as well (e.g., Gal. 1:8–9; 3:6–29).

Part 3 of this work engaged the testimony of the New Testament. First, the categorical and apparently contradictory statements—in particular, the command of Jesus to "love your enemies" (Matt. 5:44) and of Paul to "bless and curse not" (Rom. 12:14)—were addressed in their contexts and in relation to the imprecations among the psalms.

The radical command of Christ was seen not to be in utter opposition to the requirements of the Old Testament; he came not to abolish but to fulfill (Matt. 5:17). Rather, the command was a startling intensification of the love command revealed in Leviticus 19. But Jesus explicitly broadens the designation of "neighbor" to include "enemy." Enemy-love is essentially the readiness to show indiscriminate kindness, patterned after the example of the heavenly Father. Paul's blanket requirement of blessing, to the utter exclusion of cursing, was given to reveal the characteristic Christian ethic, in the context and under the heading of "genuine love" (Rom. 12:9–21). The broader resolution of the quandary aroused by this command in relation to the imprecatory psalms and even Pauline imprecations is found in the phrase, "be quick to bless, and slow to curse."

In addition, the troublesome image of *coals of fire* in Romans 12:20 was examined in context and in light of its broader biblical background and varied historical interpretations. This image is seen to be a symbol of divine judgment rather than pangs of shame or a sign of repentance. Confidence in the primarily eschatological vengeance of God stands behind the radical love command, by which Christians are called to continually and counterinstinctively extend tangible kindness to those who hate them. Assurance of God's ultimate justice (then) frees Christians to radically love (now).

Although fewer in number and generally less vivid in imagery, several examples of New Testament imprecation were cited. Nothing in these texts indicates that God disapproves of them or their call for judgment.

Of notable first mention is Christ's curse of a fig tree near the culmination of his ministry. This imprecation was a clear illustration of judgment against faithless and fruitless Israel who had stubbornly rejected the Messiah (Mark 11:14). The curse's ultimate realization was effected in the desolation of Jerusalem.

Second, the apostles uttered imprecations on several occasions—the two most significant being the Pauline and Petrine curses of condemnation on those who sought to pervert the gospel of Christ (Gal. 1:8–9; Acts 8:20). These were specifically directed against the Judaizers of Galatia and Simon the Sorcerer, respectively. Finally, from the lips of martyred saints in heaven an impassioned appeal is made for divine vengeance, which appeal bears a striking semblance to certain imprecations in the psalms (Rev. 6:10).

The New Testament data thus speaks in two directions. First, *the ethic of enemy-love and blessing is indeed intensified, and the implications of that ethic are more extensively explored and applied.* Second, *the presence of justified imprecations also insists that, in some fashion, the utterance of imprecation remains allowable within this elevated ethic of enemy-love and blessing, as it did in the imprecatory psalms.*

Whereas "love and blessing" is the dominant ethic for the believer within both testaments, "cursing and calling for divine vengeance" reflect the believer's extreme ethic. They are a legitimate resort in extreme circumstances, against the hardened, deceitful, violent, immoral, and unjust.

Christians are continually called to seek reconciliation and practice long-suffering, forgiveness, and kindness after the pattern of God. Yet there comes a point at which justice must be enacted—whether from God directly or through his representatives, such as the state and its judicial system. This response is likewise patterned after the example of God. The inhabitants of Canaan, for instance, experienced God's long-suffering grace for four hundred years. But then their iniquity became "complete," and judgment fell. Likewise, the Israelites of the Exodus, after repeated acts of rebellion and unbelief, were finally barred from entering the Promised Land.

Christ and the pious model a similar pattern in the Scriptures.

Passages, particularly in the New Testament, superficially appear to contradict—and thus supercede—the "immoderate" appeal of the imprecatory psalms. Other texts confirm use of imprecation. The frequently encountered antinomy of "loving" and "cursing" one's enemies is mysterious, yet it can be harmonized. Properly understood, these concepts complement rather than contradict one another. Indeed, in the Scriptures of both testaments two reactions toward enmity are given: one is the *characteristic* virtue of love shown by God and his people; the other ethical response is for *extreme* instances, used when God's people face sustained injustice, hardened enmity, and gross oppression.

The divine pattern exhibited is that of repeated grace; and God's people are indeed to reflect his image. Yet grace repeatedly spurned impels punishment. It is at this point, when God's people find themselves suffering from gross or sustained injustice, that they are in principle justified in calling for divine justice and appealing to divine vengeance.

The imprecatory texts, then, may recapture a recourse that has mainly been lost by God's people in the present age. When Christians are overwhelmed, the recourse is to call out to an Avenger, knowing that the Avenger will answer. These prayers, sustained in the canon, are the church's divinely appointed and modeled source of power in the midst of powerlessness.[2] In the face of severe malevolence, they are the Christian's hope that God's justice will indeed be realized—and realized not only at the end of the age (2 Thess. 1:6–10), but also in "the land of the living" (Ps. 27:13).

Thus, Christians can find in the imprecatory psalms a divinely instilled source of strength and honor and can feel permitted to use them, as appropriate, in corporate and individual worship.[3] In this, the Christian must embrace the tension inherent in reflecting both "the kindness and severity of God" (Rom. 11:22). It is a tension that previous generations of the faithful have also faced. The imprecatory psalms are a reminder that a war is raging. It is a war of opposing powers, with casualties, traitors, and triumphs. The principal weapon of that warfare is the dual-edged message of the gospel—a message not of sweet passivity, but of life and death itself.[4]

Responding to Severe Persecution

A Sermon on Psalm 83

This Sunday[1] we are participating in the International Day of Prayer for the Persecuted Church. And the question that begs to be asked is, *How are Christians to respond to severe persecution?* This question is a natural outflow from "the letters to the seven churches" that we have just looked at in Revelation 2–3. Indeed, the suffering church in many areas of our twenty-first-century world is quite similar to the suffering church in the first-century province of Asia.

The president of Turkmenistan, for example, wishes everyone to honor him like a god, to bow in front of his picture. He calls himself "the king of kings," similar to Casesar's self-adulation. And Christians in many Muslim controlled countries suffer not only severe physical persecution, but also economic oppression, similar to the situations of Smyrna and Pergamum. In their extreme poverty, there is intense pressure to convert to Islam . . . and some do. And yet most, by God's grace, stand strong, and suffer.

How are Christians to respond to severe persecution? It is a question admirably answered in Psalm 83. This psalm is known as a "communal lament." In the community of faith's extremity, this is their cry to God. It is couched in the language and historical setting of ancient Israel, but it is the cry, not fundamentally of Israel as a nation, but of Israel as the persecuted "people of God." It is the cry of the persecuted "church."

¹O God, do not keep silent;
    be not quiet, O God, be not still.
²See how your enemies are astir,
    how your foes rear their heads.
³With cunning they conspire against your people;
    they plot against those you cherish.
⁴"Come," they say, "let us destroy them as a nation,
    that the name of Israel be remembered no more."

⁵With one mind they plot together;
    they form an alliance against you—
⁶the tents of Edom and the Ishmaelites,
    of Moab and the Hagrites,
⁷Gebal, Ammon and Amalek,
    Philistia, with the people of Tyre.
⁸Even Assyria has joined them
    to lend strength to the descendants of Lot. *Selah*

⁹Do to them as you did to Midian,
    as you did to Sisera and Jabin at the river Kishon,
¹⁰who perished at Endor
    and became like refuse on the ground.
¹¹Make their nobles like Oreb and Zeeb,
    all their princes like Zebah and Zalmunna,
¹²who said, "Let us take possession
    of the pasturelands of God."

¹³Make them like tumbleweed, O my God,
    like chaff before the wind.
¹⁴As fire consumes the forest
    or a flame sets the mountains ablaze,
¹⁵so pursue them with your tempest
    and terrify them with your storm.
¹⁶Cover their faces with shame
    so that men will seek your name, O Lord.

> [17]May they ever be ashamed and dismayed;
>   may they perish in disgrace.
> [18]Let them know that you, whose name is the LORD—
>   that you alone are the Most High over all the earth.
> (NIV)

How are Christians to respond to severe persecution? We are not there . . .
yet. Although we encounter isolated cases of Christian persecution in
our country, we don't suffer like so many of our brothers and sisters
around the world—especially those under Muslim or communist regimes.
And as the Scriptures say, we are to "share in their sufferings." So this
prayer we may pray . . . for them, and also as preparation . . . for us.

First and fundamentally, we are to pray. Our instinctual reaction to
tribulation is usually retaliation, to pay back in kind what has been done
to us. But Christ has forbidden that. Another temptation in the face of
overwhelming odds is capitulation. Give in to the pressure. Give up the
faith. The psalm writer addresses a hopeless situation. His people are
encircled by nine enemy nations, some of them related to Israel and all
bent on her destruction. These countries are aided by the greatest power
in the world, Assyria (Ps. 83:4–8). But the Lord sternly warns against
capitulation.

Rather, the recourse for his people is . . . him.

Notice that the psalm opens with the plea, "O God" (v. 1). Here must
be our focus, our beginning, and end point—neither retaliation nor capitulation, but prayer.

As has been rightly stated, "Prayer is not the preparation for the battle,
prayer *is* the battle." For the battle is the Lord's, and in prayer we come
before the Lord . . . and throw the battle-ax to him. What, then, would
we do if faced with Israel's trouble?

It is ironic that Israel's trouble is the nation of Israel's problem yet
today: Philistia is the modern-day Gaza Strip. Gebal and Tyre are now
the coastal regions of Syria and Lebanon, respectively. Edom, Ammon,
Moab, and the Hagrites fall roughly within the boundaries of today's
Jordan. The Ishmaelite desert travelers were ancestors of today's Arab
kingdoms. Amalek roamed the Sinai, now in the domain of Egypt. And
Assyria is now called Iraq.

Even in this litany of perennial enemies, we must remember the redemptive thread woven throughout the Old and New Testaments: Among those who will share in the eternal presence and praises of God will be people even from among these enemies. For the redeemed of the Lord will come "from every tribe and tongue and people and nation" (Rev. 5:9). These nations are, it is true, the sworn enemies of God's people. But one of King David's mighty men was likely a Hagrite (1 Chron. 11:38). Another was an Ammonite (v. 39). Yet another was a Moabite (v. 46). Moreover, one of his officials was also a Hagrite (27:31), and another an Ishmaelite (v. 30). Philistia and Tyre will be "born again" as God's people (Ps. 87:4). Even hated Assyria and Egypt will become God's very own, on par with Israel—fully embraced into God's people (Isa. 19:24–25). Even when we rightly—as God demonstrates in his Word—pray against the enemies of God and his people, we do so remembering the redemptive constant—a sometimes faint yet continuous tone that pervades the pages of Scripture and the plan of God.

And we pray to a God who has "bound" himself to us. Their cry of desperation is framed in the language of relationship; they cry from the context of the covenant that their God will "not be silent" (Ps. 83:1). The pictures of "fire and tempest" (vv. 14–15) echo Psalm 50:3, and Psalm 50 itself centers on the covenant relationship of the God of the world with his particular people (cf. vv. 1–7). The ten enemy nations had formed an alliance—really an "anti-covenant"—against Israel (compare the expression of this in Ps. 83:5 with 2 Chron. 20; esp. vv. 10–11, 14, 29).

And yet these nations are not fundamentally *Israel's* enemies. By the psalmist's emphasis of repetition, they are *"your* enemies, *your* foes" (Ps. 83:2 emphasis added), literally, "those who hate you." They have made a covenant "against *you"* (v. 5). This equivalence can be made because they have stationed themselves "against your people, . . . against those you cherish" (v. 3).

"They are *your* enemies," God's people may rightly claim, "for they fight against *your* people."

The enemies of God's people are . . . *enemies of God.* And God's covenant "name" (vv. 16, 18) is tied to the "name" of his people (v. 4). For God has bound himself to his people in covenant. His people appeal to him out of that covenant.

This covenant relationship holds true through time, and God has shown himself true to his covenant *in* time. Indeed, this faithfulness in the past, in delivering God's people out of impossible oppressive situations, forms the basis upon which we may appeal for God's deliverance in the present. In Psalm 83, the names hark back to the days of the judges—troubled, turbulent days (vv. 9–12). This "name-dropping" is not too impressive to us, for we know so little of the Old Testament. But to the readers, these names were of supreme significance.

Jabin was a Canaanite king and Sisera his general. They oppressed God's people until the Lord delivered them, notably through a housewife, Jael, with a hammer and spike (Judg. 4–5).

Oreb, Zeeb, Zebah, and Zalmunnah were Midianite chieftains who oppressed God's people. But the Lord delivered them through a timid Gideon and a handful of Hebrews (Judg. 6–8). The odds were overwhelming, the situation hopeless. God's people were persecuted, oppressed, and distressed. But God suddenly overturned and unexpectedly toppled these oppressive regimes to deliver his people.

And so God's people recall the past as the premise for the present. They rehearse God's miraculous actions in the past as the *template* upon which he is called to action again. He has done it before; he can, and even must, do it again. And this covenant relationship holds true today. We who have bound ourselves to Christ by faith have the assurance that Christ first bound himself to us. And it is in this relationship with our Lord and Savior that we live (cf. Christ's address as covenant Lord to the seven churches, Rev. 2–3).

And we cry for deliverance in two directions—either destruction or conversion. It is interesting that this Psalm blends at least two seemingly opposing requests for divine response: destroy them—as the request begins (83:9–11), or at least terrify and shame them (vv. 13–17); *and* cause them to seek you in covenant relationship (cf. "your name, Yahweh," which corresponds to *Jesus* in New Testament perspective) and to know/acknowledge your universal sovereignty (vv. 16, 18).

Notice that verse 16b is literally "Fill their faces with shame, so that *they* will seek your name" (emphasis added). *They* refers to the same group, not two (as the NIV implies). Two requests are blended into one. Either is "okay," for either will accomplish the deliverance of God's people at God's discretion, whether through destruction, frustration, or conversion. It is either "God, convert 'em" or "God, go get 'em."

Both sides of this request for deliverance stretch our sensitivities beyond our comfort level. For we who are far from the scene of such severe persecution have a natural aversion to prayers for the destruction of our/God's enemies. In some sense, we are to love our enemies. And those who may be enmeshed in the midst of such persecution might find it difficult to plead for the conversion of their oppressors. Both stretch us. Both are right, and the results in either direction are up to God. The prayer is ours; the response is his. The pinnacle of the request in Psalm 83, however, is instructive, for it culminates with the concern for the gospel and glory of God. This is to be the ultimate purpose of our prayer, for this is what is ultimately at stake, and this is what ultimately matters.

Last November, we were appalled to hear reports of Pakistani pastor Emmanuel's martyrdom. He had just finished his sermon when armed Muslim terrorists burst into the church, stormed the pulpit, and demanded that Pastor Emmanuel throw down his Bible. When he refused, they gunned him down, along with fifteen members of his congregation. As he fell to the floor, he locked eyes with his four-year-old daughter. She survived the attack and remembers her daddy looking at her before he fell to the ground and "went to sleep" to be "in heaven with Jesus." The pastor's widow nobly, though tearfully, testifies, "Our Lord told us that in his name we would suffer. It is an honor and a privilege that my husband is a martyr for Jesus."[2]

This poignant account is just one of many. *How are Christians to respond to such severe persecution? First and fundamentally, we are to pray.* Not retaliate; not capitulate, but pray. *And we pray to a God who has bound himself in covenant to us.* He has acted in the past, and he can act in the present. And this covenant finds its focus, its greatest action—and its ironic triumph through suffering—in the cross of Christ. *And we are to pray for deliverance in two directions—either destruction or conversion.*

But the focus is, and must always be, the gospel and glory of God.

Endnotes

Introduction: Facing the Problem

1. Borrowing from the language of Ecclesiastes 3:1–8.
2. Imprecations in the Psalms, as in the rest of Scripture, are not limited to "formal curses." J. Carl Laney ably represents the breadth of definition involved in the use of the term: "An 'imprecation' is an invocation of judgment, calamity, or curse uttered against one's enemies, or the enemies of God." J. Carl Laney, "A Fresh Look at the Imprecatory Psalms," *Bibliotheca Sacra* 138 (1981): 35. And Walter Brueggemann addresses the issue broadly in terms of a "yearning for vengeance." Walter Brueggemann, *Praying the Psalms* (Winona, Minn.: Saint Mary's, 1986), 57. Both elements of "curse" and "cry for vengeance" are included as characteristic of an imprecatory psalm. So, for instance, although the bold and poignant appeal for divine recompense voiced in Psalm 137 differs markedly from the detailed litany of curses rehearsed in Psalm 109, both are universally recognized as imprecations and imprecatory psalms—indeed, they are the premier examples.
3. Partly based upon a negative reaction to the invectives hurled against their enemies by the psalmists, Hermann Gunkel asserts, "The opinion that the Old Testament is a safe guide to true religion and morality cannot any longer be maintained." Hermann Gunkel, *What Remains of the Old Testament and Other Essays,* trans. A. K. Dallas (London: Allen & Unwin, 1928), 16.
4. A theologically adequate reconciliation of the imprecatory psalms to Christian ethics must deal fairly with all of scriptural revelation. See chapter 2.

5. E.g., C. S. Lewis, *Reflections on the Psalms* (New York: Harcourt, Brace and Co., 1958); C. S. Lewis, *Christian Reflections,* ed. Walter Hooper (Grand Rapids: Eerdmans, 1967); Walter Brueggemann, *The Message of the Psalms: A Theological Commentary* (Minneapolis: Augsburg, 1984); Walter Brueggemann, *Praying the Psalms.*

6. E.g., Laney, "A Fresh Look at the Imprecatory Psalms," 35–45; Meredith G. Kline, *The Structure of Biblical Authority* (Grand Rapids: Eerdmans, 1972).

7. E.g., James E. Adams, *War Psalms of the Prince of Peace: Lessons from the Imprecatory Psalms* (Phillipsburg, N.J.: Presbyterian & Reformed, 1991); Dietrich Bonhoeffer, "A Bonhoeffer Sermon," trans. Daniel Bloesch, ed. F. Burton Nelson, *Theology Today* 38 (1982): 465–71; idem, *Psalms: The Prayer Book of the Bible,* trans. James H. Burtness (Minneapolis: Augsburg, 1970).

8. H. G. L. Peels notes that the biblical concept of vengeance "is determined by the notion of legitimate, righteous, even necessary enactment of justice by a legitimate authority." H. G. L. Peels, *The Vengeance of God: The Meaning of the Root NQM and the Function of the NQM-Texts in the Context of Divine Revelation in the Old Testament,* Oudtestamentische Studiën, ed. A. S. Van der Woude (Leiden: E. J. Brill, 1995), 31:265.

9. For instance, note the frequent pairing of "vengeance" with "recompense"— paying back what is deserved (e.g., Isa. 34:8; 35:4).

10. Cf., e.g., Deuteronomy 32:34–43; Psalms 58:10–11; 94:1–2; Isaiah 34:1–2; 59:15b–20; Luke 18:1–8; Revelation 6:10; 16:5–7; 18:4–8, 20; 19:1–2.

11. Peels, *Vengeance of God,* 31:278.

12. Though "loving-kindness" is no longer the most popular English translation for the Hebrew חֶסֶד, *hesed,* it nonetheless reflects much of the richness inherent in the term.

13. Brueggemann, *Praying the Psalms,* 62.

14. The culmination of this dual relationship, however, comes only in the age to come. God's relationship with people vis-à-vis vengeance or mercy finds its full or "perfect" realization in the eschaton, inaugurated in that great Judgment Day.

15. Edom is used in Isaiah 34 as typical of the nations (compare vv. 2, 5), the prime exhibit of the enemies of Israel. She is nearer geographically and ethnically than the great world powers; and her kinship to Israel makes the affront of her enmity the more severe.

16. Cf. Isaiah 34:2, 5. In the language of "holy war," whatever was labeled חֵרֶם,

ḥērem, was dedicated to God almost invariably for the purpose of utter annihilation.

17. Cf. the imagery that culminates in Isaiah 34:8. From the prophet's perspective, divine jealousy expressed on behalf of his covenant Bride is a virtue.

18. Raymond H. Swartzbach, "A Biblical Study of the Word 'Vengeance'," *Interpretation* 6 (1952): 457. Elmer Smick elaborates, "The Bible balances the fury of God's vengeance against the sinner with the greatness of his mercy on those whom he redeems from sin. God's vengeance must never be viewed apart from his purpose to show mercy. He is not *only* the God of wrath, but must be the God of wrath in order for his mercy to have meaning. Apart from God himself the focus of the OT is not on the objects of his vengeance but on the objects of his mercy." Elmer B. Smick, "בָּקַם," *Theological Wordbook of the Old Testament,* ed. R. Laird Harris et al. (Chicago: Moody, 1980), 2:599. Hereafter cited as *TWOT.*

19. Hans-Joachim Kraus, *Theology of the Psalms,* trans. Keith Crim (Minneapolis: Augsburg, 1986), 67.

20. As Raymond Surburg notes, "The imprecations and maledictions in the Psalter may be understood to ask God to do with the ungodly and wicked exactly what the Bible says that God has done . . . , is doing, and will do." Raymond F. Surburg, "The Interpretation of the Imprecatory Psalms," *Springfielder* 39 (1975): 99.

21. Robert Dabney notes that "righteous retribution is one of the glories of the divine character. If it is right that God should desire to exercise it, then it cannot be wrong for his people to desire him to exercise it." Robert L. Dabney, "The Christian's Duty Towards His Enemies," in *Discussions by Robert L. Dabney,* ed. C. R. Vaughan (Richmond: Presbyterian Committee of Publication, 1890), 1:715. Similarly, J. W. Beardslee notes that as the soul comes to stand where God stands, as it becomes progressively conformed to the image of its Creator (Col. 3:10), it will feel as God feels and speak as God speaks. Thus, not only will there be a deep abhorrence of sin, but there will also be a righteous indignation against the willful and persistent wrongdoer. J. W. Beardslee, "The Imprecatory Element in the Psalms," *Presbyterian and Reformed Review* 8 (1897): 504.

22. The radical demands of love that our Lord places on his followers are patterned after the example of God, notably portrayed in Matthew 5:44–45 and Luke 6:35–36: "Love your enemies . . . so that you may be sons of your

Father who is in heaven"; and "Love your enemies . . . and you will be sons of the Most High, because he is kind to the ungrateful and evil. Be compassionate, just as also your Father is compassionate."

23. "Give place to [God's] wrath . . . Vengeance is mine; I will repay" (Rom. 12:19b-c).

24. "He is God's servant, an avenger for wrath . . ." (Rom. 13:4c). In Romans 12:19–20, Christians are forbidden to take revenge but are rather to defer to God's wrath and do good. This is to be our personal ethic and is in concord with the "second greatest commandment," "Do not take revenge . . . but love your neighbor as yourself" (Lev. 19:18). In this way, we "conquer evil with good" (Rom. 12:21b). But in 13:4, governmental ethics is the ethics of "revenge"—as servants of God's wrath on this very "evil." The state is entrusted with taking revenge, and we are to defer to that wrath and do good. Just as we are *not* to take revenge and *are* to do good, knowing that God will take vengeance on the day of wrath on all who remain unrepentant of their evil (Rom. 12:19–20), so the state *is to take revenge and to commend the good* we do (Rom. 13:3–4). Whereas the Christian is to be fundamentally governed by the principle of love, the state is to be fundamentally governed by the principle of recompense: punishing evil; promoting good.

25. See especially Numbers 14:22–23, in which the Israelites are said to have tested Yahweh "ten times" and thus treated him with contempt.

26. After enduring two centuries of worship of the golden calves at Bethel and Dan, as instituted by Jeroboam (1 Kings 12:26–13:2), and the increasing compromise to pagan ways and the worship of Baal, as instituted by Ahab (1 Kings 16:30–33), God said, in essence, "No further!" Hosea speaks, for example, of Israel's imminent destruction, using the image of a "vulture [poised] over the house of Yahweh" (8:1). Her "days of punishment/ recompense have come" (9:7). God will "remember their wickedness" (8:13; cf. Jer. 14:10 with 31:34, in which God promises to "remember their sin no more"). Their sins have reached the point at which God has "hated/rejected" the Israelites (Hos. 9:15, 17). Because of their sins, they will be subject to the depth of human depravity, "their little ones dashed to the ground, their pregnant women ripped open" (13:16). They will "return to Egypt" (8:13; 9:3; 11:5) in a shocking reversal of Israel's redemption in the Exodus (although even here hope is held out, 11:11). They will no longer be shown

compassion (1:6), no longer be called "My people" (1:9). Yahweh will no longer be their "I Am" (although Hosea extends hope in 2:1–3; 2:14–23; ch. 3). For similar expression of the severity of God toward his people for their stubborn sin, see Jeremiah 7:16; 11:14; 14:11. It is significant that Yahweh tells Jeremiah *not* to pray for them.

27. ". . . 'Yahweh, Yahweh, the compassionate and gracious God, slow to anger and abounding in loving-kindness and faithfulness, maintaining loving-kindness to thousands, and forgiving iniquity, rebellion, and sin. Yet he by no means leaves the guilty unpunished'" (Exod. 34:6–7a).

28. Indeed, if the fullness of the character of Christ is to be known, the prime exhibit in Hebrews 12:2–3 of enduring the cross and opposition from sinful men must be expanded to include his symbolic curse on the nation who rejected him (Mark 11:12–21)—a curse realized in that generation in the desolation of Jerusalem.

29. This is a judgment in which Christ, the "Son of Man," participates (Rev. 14:14–16).

30. Notice here how the Song of Moses—the song of divine vengeance—is equated in some measure with the Song of Christ the Lamb.

31. Surburg, "The Interpretation of the Imprecatory Psalms," 100.

32. In the progress of revelation, the New Testament reflects a development, not in morality per se, but in the way the divinely ordained ethic is lived out in daily life. Steadfast endurance under unjust suffering for the sake of Christ and after the pattern of Christ, entrusting both temporal and eschatological judgment to God, becomes a more predominant theme in the New Testament, whereas it is more restrained in the Old Testament. The New Testament epistle of 1 Peter, for example, which addresses Christians in the context of persecution and advocates endurance in the midst of suffering, speaks nothing of imprecating one's enemies. Rather, it heralds the importance of patiently awaiting the return of Christ the Judge. This is significant, in that it starkly underscores what is to be considered the characteristic Christian ethic and approach to persecution and oppression. First Peter 2:18–23, for example, adjures Christian slaves to endure unjust beatings, based on the example of Christ, entrusting their lives and the realization of justice to the God of justice. Blessing and endurance characterize the Christian life (cf. 3:9; 4:12–19) to which the epistle speaks, and, in principle, is the dominant mood of the New Testament and also (in a more subdued

tone) of the Old Testament. The imprecatory passages, however, supplement this general tenor, articulating the minor—yet complementary—ethic evidenced in extreme instances.

33. This includes 5:10; 6:10; 7:6, 9, 15–16; 9:19–20; 10:15; 17:13; 28:4; 31:17–18; 35:1, 4–6, 8, 19, 24–26; 40:14–15; 52:5; 54:5; 55:9, 15; 56:7; 58:6–10; 59:5, 11–13; 68:1–2, 30; 69:22–25, 27–28; 70:2–3; 71:13; 74:11, 22–23; 79:6, 10, 12; 83:9, 11, 13–18; 94:1–2; 104:35; 109:6–15, 17–20, 29; 129:5–8; 137:7–9; 139:19, 21–22; 140:8–11; 141:10; 143:12. Those psalms which may be rightly deemed "imprecatory" (i.e., whose characterizing element is the imprecations or cries for divine vengeance) are better limited to fourteen: Psalms 7; 35; 55; 58; 59; 69; 79; 83; 94; 109; 129; 137; 139; and 140.

34. Psalm 58 contains a series of graphic imprecations against what is deemed a societal enemy—judges who have become blatantly unjust, deceitful, and violent. In it, appeal is made to the true Judge to mete out true justice swiftly and decisively. Under this umbrella Psalm 94 may be subsumed, for it involves the cry for divine vengeance from the "Judge of the earth" (v. 2) against a corrupt and oppressive judicial throne (vv. 5–6, 20–21). Psalm 137 is a shockingly emotive cry from the bowels of the exiled remnant against those who had, with such carnage and cruelty, devastated Judea. Stationed under 137, several psalms call for divine vengeance upon a national or community enemy, uttered either by the community itself, or by an individual speaking from the community's perspective (Pss. 68; 74; 79; 83; 129). The majority of the imprecatory psalms, however, are situated against a personal enemy, or a collective enemy viewed from the perspective of the individual (notably, David). The one usually identified as most offensive in this category, is Psalm 109. Under this plethora of imprecations, the various and remaining personal imprecatory psalms may be comprehended (Pss. 5; 6; 7; 9; 10; 17; 28; 31; 35; 40; 52; 54; 55; 56; 59; 69; 70; 71; 104; 139; 140; 141; 143).

35. There are dynamic tensions in Scripture that people of both scholarship and piety will never finally understand or be able to fully reconcile. At such points of mystery, which serve to divide the finite from the divine, our approach must be one of (eventual) submission and conscientious obedience (cf. Deut. 29:29).

36. E.g., in Revelation 1:17 Jesus is, by ascription, equated with Yahweh (alluding to Isa. 44:6; 48:12); and in Revelation 21:3, 7 God proclaims the culmi-

nation of the defining covenant declaration (cf. Gen.17:7–8; Lev. 26:11–12; 2 Sam. 7:14; Jer. 31:33).

37. E.g., 1 Peter 2:9 speaks of the New Testament church in language drawn from that inaugural declaration of Old Testament Israel as the people of God (Exod. 19:5–6); Galatians 3:29 attests that those who are in Christ are heirs of the Abrahamic promise; Romans 4 affirms Abraham as our father in the faith and the exemplar of our faith.

38. E.g., in Matthew 22:36–40 Christ distills the essence of the Old Testament commands as that of love for God and love for one's neighbor (quoting from Deut. 6:5 and Lev. 19:18); in 1 John 4:21, this same dual-faceted command is given to govern God's new covenant people; in Galatians 5:13–6:2, the "law of Christ" is linked to this very "law of love."

39. E.g., in Matthew 5:17 Christ asserts that he came not to abolish the Old Testament but to fulfill it; 2 Corinthians 1:20 teaches that all God's promises find their ultimate realization in Christ—and thus also to those united to him; Revelation 21–22 and Genesis 1–3 together form an overarching inclusio to the Scriptures in their entirety.

Chapter 1: Unsatisfactory Solutions

1. C. S. Lewis, *Reflections on the Psalms* (New York: Harcourt, Brace & Co., 1958), 20–21.

2. Ibid., 21–22.

3. C. S. Lewis, *Christian Reflections,* ed. Walter Hooper (Grand Rapids: Eerdmans, 1967), 120–21.

4. Lewis, *Reflections on the Psalms,* 33.

5. Ibid., 22.

6. A certain ambiguity exists in the use of the introductory *lamedh* (ל) in the superscriptions of the psalms. Indeed, its fluidity of meaning is patently evidenced by the threefold use in Psalm 18:1: *"for* the choir director, *of* David, the servant of Yahweh, who spoke *to* Yahweh" (emphasis added). Granting this, however, the traditional understanding of the ל in, for example, לְדָוִד, *lĕdāwid,* "of David," is adopted herein as the *lamedh* of authorship for the following reasons: (1) The extended superscription found in Psalm 18:1 makes the matter of authorship explicit. And it is likely that *"of* David" is the abbreviated form of the longer and frequent "a psalm of David" (cf. Hab. 3:1, "a

prayer *of* Habakkuk"). (2) Such an understanding is consonant with David's reputation as both musician and composer (e.g., 2 Sam. 23:1; Amos 6:5; 1 Chron. 15–16). And both Christ and the apostles considered David himself to be the author of those psalms that bore this imprint (e.g., Mark 12:35–37; Acts 2:25–35). (3) Such is the customary idiom in other Semitic dialects, and numerous early Hebrew inscriptions on personal articles evidence a similar use—the *lamedh* of ownership (i.e., "belonging to").

7. This is not to assert that David was in any way a stranger to sin and rebellion. But the governing principle of his life was חֶסֶד, *ḥesed*, "loving-kindness."

8. Thus, if the imprecatory psalms are considered sinful, their very prominence and prevalence in the collection of Davidic psalms contradicts what is characteristically known of him elsewhere in Scripture.

9. E.g., after having been hounded relentlessly by the madly jealous King Saul, David finally had the choice opportunity to dispatch him while he was ignobly positioned in the cave in which David and his confederates were hiding. David's conscience, however, would not allow him to strike down "Yahweh's anointed." After Saul had gone back to his troops, David called out to him from the cave, "May Yahweh judge between me and you. And may Yahweh avenge me for what you have done, but my hand will not be against you" (1 Sam. 24:12). And Saul's response is enlightening: "When a man finds his enemy, does he send him on his way unharmed? May Yahweh reward you well for the way you treated me today" (v. 19).

10. But, it may well be asked, how can divine inspiration be applied to the Psalms, which, by their very nature, are the response of men back *to* God. How can the words of men to God be the Word of God to men? In what sense, and to what extent, can we admit that they bear the stamp of the Holy Spirit? To these questions is readily admitted a measure of mystery. But the larger testimony of Scripture as well the history of God's people (including the process of canonization) witness that the Psalter, in its entirety, is included under the aegis of "God-breathed" (2 Tim. 3:16)—by the Holy Spirit through godly men (cf., e.g., Heb. 3:7–10, in which a quotation from Ps. 95:7b–11 is introduced by, "as the Holy Spirit says").

11. Lewis, *Reflections on the Psalms,* 19.

12. George S. Gunn, *God in the Psalms* (Edinburgh: Saint Andrew, 1956), 99 (emphasis in original). Similarly, Chalmers Martin observes that the psalms included for use in the public worship of God contain an implicit claim

that the poet's expressed feelings are "in some sense true and right, such as others should sympathize with and, it may be, adopt as their own." Chalmers Martin, "The Imprecations in the Psalms," *Princeton Theological Review* 1 (1903): 540. Indeed, the sheer quantity of the cries for divine vengeance in the Psalms calls into question the view that they are not, in some measure at least, exemplary.

13. As L. Russ Bush notes, the "prominence of the imprecatory material is an internal evidence that the biblical writers themselves did not see any inconsistency in their devotion to God and their call for judgment upon the wicked." L. Russ Bush, "Does God Inspire Imprecation? Divine Authority and Ethics in the Psalms" (Evangelical Philosophical Society Presidential Address, November 16, 1990), 6.

14. Although it may be argued that such expressions were retained to show succeeding generations that all things may be rightly brought to Yahweh in prayer—even our rage and revenge—this would have to be inferred, for such a limit and intent is nowhere explicitly stated.

15. Gunn, *God in the Psalms*, 99.

16. Walter Brueggemann, *Praying the Psalms* (Winona, Minn.: Saint Mary's, 1986), 68 (emphasis in original).

17. Ibid. (emphasis in original).

18. Walter Brueggemann, *The Message of the Psalms: A Theological Commentary* (Minneapolis: Augsburg, 1984), 85.

19. This conviction is echoed by Peter Craigie, that although the sentiments expressed in the imprecatory psalms "are in themselves evil, they are a part of the life of the soul which is bared before God in worship and prayer." Peter C. Craigie, *Psalms 1–50*, Word Biblical Commentary, ed. David A. Hubbard and Glenn W. Barker (Waco, Tex.: Word, 1983), 19:41. Erich Zenger likewise notes that the imprecatory psalms bring us face to face with "the fundamental biblical conviction that in prayer we may say everything, literally everything, if only we say it to GOD." Erich Zenger, *A God of Vengeance? Understanding the Psalms of Divine Wrath*, trans. Linda M. Maloney (Louisville: Westminster John Knox, 1996), 79. But the question may rightly be asked, *Why are there* so many *imprecations in the psalms?* If such calls for divine vengeance are to be construed as expressions of the faithful believer's "dark side"—even if intended as a teaching tool—how is the inclusion of such a disproportionately large contingent of "curses" to be explained?

20. Cf. Luke 12:49, "I have come to cast *fire* on the earth, and how I wish it were already kindled!" (emphasis added; cf. the impassioned "woe" of Christ uttered against Judas in Matt. 26:24).

21. In addition, an instance of actual imprecation from the lips of our Lord is recorded in Mark 11:12–14, 20–21 (cf. Matt. 21:18–20). As both the near context and the larger development of the Gospel elucidate, Christ's cursing of the fig tree is a not-so-veiled imprecation against faithless and fruitless Israel—an Israel who had so stubbornly rejected him.

22. Roy B. Zuck, "The Problem of the Imprecatory Psalms" (Th.M. thesis, Dallas Theological Seminary, 1957), 73. Hammond similarly estimates "that prayers for the temporal and even capital punishment of the wicked, while unlawful and unjustifiable on the lips of Christian men, were nevertheless, under certain conditions, perfectly lawful and perfectly natural on the part of those to whom life and immortality and a judgment *to come* had not been brought to light." Joseph Hammond, "The Vindictive Psalms Vindicated: Part 4," *Expositor* 3 (1876): 452 (emphasis in original). This assertion loses force, however, when one encounters the same or similar imprecations in the New Testament.

23. Zuck, "Problem of the Imprecatory Psalms," 70. He adds, "The difference in the dispensations of law and grace demands an acceptance of the fact that the moral standards of the Old Testament were not on the high level of that of the New Testament. For example, love for one's enemies as found in the New Testament is *foreign* to Old Testament morality." Ibid., 73 (emphasis added). Although it is rightly espoused that the New Testament ethic of enemy-love is more explicit and given greater emphasis, and the ramifications of that ethic are more widely explored and applied, such ethic is not wholly new. Indeed, the concept of enemy-love is not "foreign" to Old Testament morality; rather it is latent or subdued, finding full flower in Christ.

24. Ibid., 60 (emphasis in original).

25. Thus, although the term רֵג, *gēr*, speaks generically of a "resident alien," in this context is the added nuance of a basic and natural enmity as well. Israel entered Egypt on friendly terms, but the enmity of denigration and oppression of slavery characterized their "sojourn" in Egypt. Yahweh forbids that the kind of mistreatment suffered by Israelites at the hands of Egyptians should be perpetrated by Israelites against the aliens in Israel's midst (cf. Deut. 10:19).

26. The Arameans of Elisha's day were the epitome of the enemy. And Naaman's unnamed slave girl, acquired in a raid against Israel, surprisingly sought the welfare of her foreign master—the Aramean army commander. Elisha likewise responded to his need with grace.

27. This account of kindness—of love—toward one's enemies, is one of the most dramatic in all of Scripture. When the Israelite people of Dothan were hopelessly caged by the Arameans, the prophet Elisha prayed that God would blind the eyes of the enemy army. By a ruse, he then led them to the Israelite capital of Samaria. Once inside "their" enemy territory, their sight was returned, and the Israelite king asked Elisha if he should kill them. Elisha instead directed the king to give them food and water and send them back unharmed. This mercy inaugurated a time of peace with Aram.

28. This example of Yahweh's "unexpected" compassion toward the Assyrians—his inveterate adversaries and the oppressors of his people—is contrasted with the unbecoming response of Jonah.

29. F. G. Hibbard, *The Psalms Chronologically Arranged, with Historical Introductions; and a General Introduction to the Whole Book,* 5th ed. (New York: Carlton & Porter, 1856), 107.

30. J. W. Beardslee, "The Imprecatory Element in the Psalms," *Presbyterian and Reformed Review* 8 (1897): 496 (emphasis in original). To his credit, Zuck insists upon this very issue ("Problem of the Imprecatory Psalms," 57), thus largely concurring with the present argument. Notably, Revelation 22:18–19, the culmination of revelation's progress, issues grave warnings in a manner reminiscent of certain ancient Near Eastern curses.

31. Cf. Romans 13:8–10; Galatians 5:13–14; 6:2; 1 John 4:20–21. This is the fundamental constant: a wholehearted love of God and neighbor. As has been recognized for some time, these two commands are the essence of the Decalogue, the heart of the Law of Moses. A different level of emphasis is placed in regard to the Christian's status toward his enemies (i.e., loving vs. hating them), due in large part to the different stage of the outworking of God's plan among and through his people; but a love of neighbor, expressed in kindness, which included one's enemies in their time of need, was both commanded and modeled in the Old Testament.

32. Yet even to those who would have destroyed God's people, love/kindness was demonstrated in certain discrete instances.

33. Cf., e.g., Matthew 5:43–44; 1 Peter 2:21–23.

34. Martin, "Imprecations in the Psalms," 548.

35. Robert Althann similarly proposes that "a Christian re-reading turns the execration of individuals into a denunciation of the unjust situation provoked by them." Robert Althann, "The Psalms of Vengeance Against Their Ancient Near Eastern Background," *Journal of Northwest Semitic Languages* 18 (1992): 10.

36. E.g., C. S. Lewis, in reflecting upon the imprecations in the psalms, denies that God looks upon the psalmists' enemies as they do (i.e., with hatred). While he asserts that God doubtless "has for the sin of those enemies just the implacable hostility which the poets express," he maintains that such hatred is directed "not to the sinner but to the sin." Lewis, *Reflections on the Psalms*, 32.

37. No matter how horrible this concept and its imagery may seem, it is, nonetheless, the clear teaching of Scripture and is to the glory of the fully-orbed character of God. From the lips of the "gentle and humble" Jesus himself, for example (cf. Matt. 11:29), come these disturbing words: "If your eye causes you to sin, pluck it out. It is better for you to enter one-eyed into the kingdom of God than having two eyes to be thrown into Gehenna, where their worm does not die, and the fire is not extinguished" (Mark 9:47–48). Christ here draws from the closing verse of Isaiah, in its contrast between the final estate of the righteous and the wicked. The righteous are said to worship Yahweh continually. But in addition, "they will go out and look upon the dead bodies of the people who rebelled against me: Their worm does not die, and their fire is not extinguished; and they will be an abhorrence to all flesh" (Isa. 66:24). This stark imagery of a "perpetual death" of terror and pain rises to the limits of language in its description of hell. Furthermore, and quite disturbing from the present vantage point (although at that time Christians will more fully join the passions of God), Revelation 14:9–11 describes this eternal torment as *in the presence* of heaven: "If anyone worships the beast and his image and receives the mark on his forehead or on his hand, then he will drink of the wine of the rage of God, which has been poured full strength into the cup of his wrath, and he will be tormented in fire and sulfur before the holy angels and before the Lamb. And the smoke of their torment rises for ever and ever."

38. John L. McKenzie, "The Imprecations of the Psalter," *American Ecclesiastical Review* 111 (1944): 91. It is for such reason as this, he argues, that law-abiding citizens may consent to the execution of a murderer—not because of the pleasure his killing gives them, but because his death restores the

order of justice that his crime has violated. Moreover, speaking out of the context of the Second World War, he contends that "we would not carry on the war if we did not regard our enemies as evil and desire efficaciously to inflict evil upon them. This is a species of hatred." Ibid., 90.

39. Ibid., 92–93 (emphasis in original).

40. Reading פֶּחָמֵי, *paḥămê*, "coals of" (cf. Symmachus' ἄνθρακας, *anthrakas*), in lieu of the MT's פַּחִים, *paḥîm*, "snares." The difficulty of the MT as it stands is exacerbated in that it portrays an unparalleled metaphor for judgment and evidently arose due to an accidental transposition of the *yod* and *mem* in a consonantal text. Moreover, the adopted reading yields better line symmetry (5:4) than that of the MT (3:6), which reads instead (supported by the LXX), "He will rain on the wicked snares; fire and sulphur and a scorching wind will be the portion of their cup."

41. John Piper, *The Pleasures of God: Meditations on God's Delight in Being God* (Portland, Ore.: Multnomah, 1991), 66.

42. Humans are created in God's image (and thus are to show his image, Gen. 1:26–28). Christians are being renewed in that image (Col. 3:10), so they are to imitate Christ (as modeled by Paul, 1 Cor. 11:1).

43. In this regard it is instructive to place that "patently offensive outburst" of David, uttered in Psalm 139:19, 21–22, alongside the description expressed in Psalm 5:5–7 of God's character and sentiment toward the wicked. David is seeking but to reflect God's character and echo his sentiment.

> [5]Surely, you are not a God who takes pleasure in wickedness;
>> evil cannot dwell with you.
> [6]The boastful cannot stand before your eyes;
>> you hate all who practice iniquity.
> [7]You destroy those who tell lies;
>> bloodthirsty and deceitful men Yahweh abhors. (5:5–7)

> [19]If only you would slay the wicked, O God!
>> Away from me, you bloodthirsty men!
> [21]Do I not hate those who hate you, O Yahweh,
>> and loathe those who rise up against you?
> [22]I hate them with perfect hatred;
>> I count them my enemies. (139:19, 21–22)

44. Cf., e.g., John 4:4–42 and 8:2–11 with Matthew 11:20–24 and 23:1–39.

45. Raymond F. Surburg, "The Interpretation of the Imprecatory Psalms," *Springfielder* 39 (1975): 100.

46. This creative tension of loving yet hating the hardened sinner is ably represented by Thrupp: "Imprecations of judgment on the wicked *on the hypothesis of their continued impenitence* are not inconsistent with simultaneous efforts to bring them to repentance; and Christian charity itself can do no more than labour for the sinner's conversion. The law of holiness requires us to pray for the fires of divine retribution: the law of love to seek meanwhile to rescue the brand from the burning." Joseph Francis Thrupp, *An Introduction to the Study and Use of the Psalms* (Cambridge: Macmillan, 1860), 2:202 (emphasis in original).

47. Surburg, "Interpretation of the Imprecatory Psalms," 100. Indeed, in God's economy, "the wages of sin is death" for the sinner (Rom. 6:23). And for all whose sins are not wiped out in the cross of Christ, they remain under the condemnation of God (John 3:18, 36).

48. In many ways, this "hating" is a relational term, realized as a distancing of oneself from the wicked: notice how David prefaces his remark of hatred with, "Away from me!" (Ps. 139:19). Additionally, the godly Judean king, Jehoshaphat, was chided by Jehu the seer, following his return from the ill-fated war alliance with the wicked Israelite king, Ahab, for "loving those who hate Yahweh" (2 Chron. 19:2; i.e., allying himself with one so opposed to God, passively affirming his wickedness).

49. J. Carl Laney, "A Fresh Look at the Imprecatory Psalms," *Bibliotheca Sacra* 138 (1981): 41–42. And upon this basis, "David had a perfect right . . . to pray that God would effect what He had promised." Ibid., 42.

50. Ibid., 44. He also dismisses the cry for divine vengeance of the martyrs in heaven (Rev. 6:10). He believes that it does not apply to the church age.

51. According to the argument of Paul in Galatians 3, in which he plays off the ambiguity latent in the collective singular σπέρμα (*sperma*, Gal. 3:16)/זֶרַע (*zeraʿ*; Gen. 12:7; 13:15; 22:18), Messiah Jesus is "the Seed" *par excellence,* of whom the covenant promise was made—as interpreted through the development of the promise in the Davidic and new covenants. As Matthew 1:1 presents him, he is *the* Son of David and *the* Son of Abraham. Both Solomon, the initial fulfillment of the Davidic covenant (2 Sam. 7:12–16), and Isaac, the initial fulfillment of the Abrahamic covenant (Gen. 21:12), are

swallowed up in Christ. He is the "yes" of all God's promises (2 Cor. 1:20); thus, all who share in Christ share in the promises. This inclusion of all races and classes into the Abrahamic promise as his "seed" through Christ "the Seed" comes to a focus in Galatians 3:26–29.

52. This blessing of the covenant is articulated as the blessing of life, of sonship, and of the Spirit (Gal. 3:14, 26; 4:4–7); and the curse is the curse of death and condemnation (Gal. 3:10–13). The distilled argument here is that the Gentiles through faith in Christ, the Seed of Abraham, fully partake in the covenant made to Abraham. And although the blessings of the covenant explicitly mentioned by Paul are spiritual in nature, this is not meant to categorically exclude the more "physical" elements of the Abrahamic covenant. Rather, it is for the sake of emphasizing the fundamental issues of the promise in the progress of revelation—which issues are most germane to his argument.

53. Meredith G. Kline, *The Structure of Biblical Authority* (Grand Rapids: Eerdmans, 1972), 160.

54. Ibid.

55. Ibid., 161. For Kline, it is only the principle of intrusion that makes the destruction of physical enemies in the old covenant, and the cries for such in the Psalms, permissible. For in the consummation, "no longer will there be the possibility that the enemy of the saint is the elect of God." Ibid., 162.

56. Harry Mennega, "The Ethical Problem of the Imprecatory Psalms" (Th.M. thesis, Westminster Theological Seminary, 1959), 87. Thomas, in seeking to justify the prayer of the martyrs in Revelation 6, asserts that they are able to pray this way because they had been given some special revelation that identified the reprobate—a knowledge possessed only in divine perspective. Robert L. Thomas, "The Imprecatory Prayers of the Apocalypse," *Bibliotheca Sacra* 126 (1969): 129–30. This, however, merely evades the issue.

57. Divine inspiration of the Psalter, which is explicitly affirmed, does not entail a special knowledge of the human author into God's secret decree.

58. Zuck, "The Problem of the Imprecatory Psalms," 64, 66.

59. Mennega, "The Ethical Problem of the Imprecatory Psalms," 94.

60. Although this method is by no means foolproof (cf. the example of Saul-Paul), it is, nonetheless, the Christian's sure and proverbial guide in daily living.

61. Cf. Calvin, who, in commenting on 2 Timothy 4:14, adjures Christians to

pronounce sentence "only against reprobates, who, by their impiety, give evidence that such is their true character." John Calvin, *Commentaries on the Epistles to Timothy, Titus, and Philemon,* trans. William Pringle (1556; reprint, Grand Rapids: Eerdmans, 1948), 269.

62. H. G. L. Peels, *The Vengeance of God: The Meaning of the Root* NQM *and the Function of the* NQM-*Texts in the Context of Divine Revelation in the Old Testament,* Oudtestamentische Studiën, ed. A. S. van der Woude (Leiden: E. J. Brill, 1995), 31:246.

63. Ibid., 245.

64. Ibid., 246. Similarly, Longman argues that since the Christian's warfare is against Satan and the spiritual forces of evil, his or her curses are to be reserved for them. Tremper Longman III, *How to Read the Psalms* (Downers Grove, Ill.: InterVarsity, 1988), 139.

65. E.g., Deuteronomy 32:16–17; Joshua 24:14–15; 1 Samuel 4–6; 1 Kings 17–18.

66. E.g., Isaiah 2; 4; 11; 19:16–25; 24–27; 34–35; 60–62; 65:17–66:24.

67. As I. Howard Marshall notes, this "may sound like profanity, but is precisely what the Greek says." I. Howard Marshall, *The Acts of the Apostles,* Tyndale New Testament Commentaries, ed. R. V. G. Tasker (Leicester: Inter-Varsity, 1983), 159.

68. It is of interest to note that Jesus' words are more directly (although not exclusively) pointed toward the Romans rather than the hardened and antagonistic Jewish religious leaders. For those, Jesus had a different sentence (cf. Matt. 23). The antecedent of "they" in Luke 23:33 is the Romans who crucified him in verse 32; and in verse 33b, it is the Romans again who are observed to divide up his clothes. In contrast, the echo of Christ's words on the lips of the dying Stephen are directed toward religious Jews. Their level of "stubbornness" (Acts 7:51), however, is apparently deemed to be of a different caliber than their earlier counterparts (cf. Acts 6:9; 7:59–60). This dynamic interplay of responses to enmity between those who are seen as hardened enemies and those considered more transiently so is illustrated well by Paul's words in 2 Timothy 4:14–16 regarding Alexander the coppersmith on the one hand and those who had deserted him at his time of desperate need on the other. Of the former he avers, "The Lord (i.e., Jesus—2 Tim. 4:8) will repay him for what he has done"; whereas concerning the latter he pleads, "May it not be counted against them"—reminiscent of the dying words of both Stephen and our Lord.

69. Here, in particular, this cry of the martyred saints *in heaven* for divine vengeance is in language strikingly reminiscent of the imprecatory psalms (cf. especially Ps. 79:10).

70. James E. Adams, *War Psalms of the Prince of Peace: Lessons from the Imprecatory Psalms* (Phillipsburg, N.J.: Presbyterian & Reformed, 1991), 21. With regard to Psalm 83, Adams asks, "Without assistance how can we ever righteously pray this prayer? I answer this question unequivocally: *We never can!* We cannot pray this prayer on our own." Ibid., 56.

71. Ibid., 33.

72. Ibid.

73. Dietrich Bonhoeffer, *Psalms: The Prayer Book of the Bible,* trans. J. H. Burtness (Minneapolis: Augsburg, 1970), 18.

74. Ibid., 19.

75. Ibid., 21.

76. Ibid., 58–60.

77. Cf., e.g., 2 Thessalonians 1:5–10; John 3:16–18, 36; Revelation 14:9–11; 20:15.

78. In the final analysis, this position both overstates David's typological function and understates David's historical situation.

79. Psalm 137 dates from the Babylonian exile; Psalms 74, 79, and 83 list Asaph as author; and Psalms 71, 94, 104, and 129 are anonymous.

80. To Bonhoeffer, although not all (even imprecatory) psalms are Davidic, the entire Psalter is "decisively bound up with the name of David." Bonhoeffer, *Psalms,* 20. However true this characterization, his position is dependent, not on a generic association, but on the genetic and typological link of historical David to historical Jesus, rendering the legitimacy of this extrapolation invalid.

81. With the exception of Brueggemann and those aligned with his position.

82. The Christian life includes "speaking to one another with 'psalms'" (Eph. 5:19).

83. McKenzie insists that "when we recite these Psalms as a part of the official prayer of the Church, we may recite them with all the fervor in the sense intended by the Holy Spirit who inspired them." McKenzie, "The Imprecations of the Psalter," 96. In a kindred spirit, Dabney maintains that "the inspired men of both Testaments felt and expressed moral indignation against wrong-doers, and a desire for their proper retribution at the hand of God. This admission must also be successfully defended, which, it is

believed, can be done in perfect consistency with that spirit of merciful forbearance and love for the persons of enemies which both Testaments alike inculcate." Robert L. Dabney, "The Christian's Duty Towards His Enemies," in *Discussions by Robert L. Dabney*, ed. C. R. Vaughan (Richmond: Presbyterian Committee of Publication, 1890), 1:711.

84. Martin Luther, *Luther's Works*, vol. 21: *The Sermon on the Mount and the Magnificat*, ed. J. Pelikan, trans. J. Pelikan, A. T. W. Steinhaeuser (St. Louis: Concordia, 1956), 1100.

Chapter 2: Curse in Its Cultural Context

1. By the term *curse* in this context, we are to understand not the profane oath or interjectory exclamation, "but rather the deliberate, considered expression of a wish that evil befall another." Stanley Gevirtz, "West-Semitic Curses and the Problem of the Origins of Hebrew Law," *Vetus Testamentum* 11 (1961): 140.

2. H. G. L. Peels, *The Vengeance of God: The Meaning of the Root NQM and the Function of the NQM-Texts in the Context of Divine Revelation in the Old Testament*, Oudtestamentische Studiën, ed. A. S. van der Woude (Leiden: E. J. Brill, 1995), 31:237.

3. Josef Scharbert, "ארר," *Theological Dictionary of the Old Testament*, trans. J. T. Willis, ed. G. Johannes Botterweck and Helmer Ringgren, rev. ed. (Grand Rapids: Eerdmans, 1977), 1:416. Hereafter cited as *TDOT*.

4. Peels, *Vengeance of God*, 238.

5. See Robert Althann, "The Psalms of Vengeance Against Their Ancient Near Eastern Background," *Journal of Northwest Semitic Languages* 18 (1992): 3–4.

6. Scharbert, "ארר," 1:417–18.

7. See John H. Walton, *Ancient Israelite Literature in Its Cultural Context* (Grand Rapids: Zondervan, 1989), 104. The structure of Deuteronomy as a whole follows this basic covenant pattern. And the Song of Moses (Deut. 32) in particular fits into the "witness" category, for it affirms Yahweh's ability to enforce the terms of the covenant. Of particular significance are verses 39–43, in which Yahweh takes an oath to exact vengeance on behalf of his people.

8. James B. Pritchard, ed., *Ancient Near Eastern Texts Relating to the Old Testament*, 3d ed. with supplement (Princeton, N.J.: Princeton University Press,

1969), 205. Hereafter cited as *ANET.* "When a curse was pronounced it often comprised in its malediction the whole activity of a man's life. His every work and interest were placed under a ban. Not only the man himself but also his seed was doomed to destruction." Samuel A. B. Mercer, "The Malediction in Cuneiform Inscriptions," *Journal of the American Oriental Society* 34 (1914): 302.

9. As Delbert Hillers observes, none of these parallels appears to be the product of "simple copying, but the possibility of influence of treaty-curses on Israelite literature, or of mutual influence, or of dependence on common sources, cannot be disregarded." Delbert R. Hillers, *Treaty-Curses and the Old Testament Prophets, Biblica et orientalia* 16 (Rome: Pontifical Biblical Institute, 1964), 78. Rather, "the point to be grasped is that both in Israel and elsewhere there were living and primarily oral traditions of curses on which writers and speakers might draw for various purposes, either leaving the material as they found it or recasting it into their own style." Ibid., 42. Kandy Sutherland agrees: "Parallels in general may be explained by the accessibility of a traditional set of curses. These curses afforded the prospect of a gathering and adaptation of the maledictions in order to fit a particular situation or need. Similarities found between Deuteronomy 28, Leviticus 26, and some of the ancient Near Eastern treaties offer evidence of the combination and reworking of traditional curses in order to address specific situations." Kandy Maria Queen Sutherland, "The Futility Curse in the Old Testament" (Ph.D. diss., Southern Baptist Theological Seminary, 1982), 153–54.

Further support for this interpretation of the comparative evidence may be seen in the similarity between the futility curses engraved on the Tell Fekherye royal statue, the Sefire I treaty, and Deuteronomy 28:17–18. The Tell Fekherye statue threatens, "May one hundred ewes suckle a lamb but let it not be sated, may one hundred cows suckle a calf but let it not be sated, may one hundred women suckle a child but let it not be sated, may one hundred women bake bread in an oven but let them not fill it." Jonas C. Greenfield and Aaron Shaffer, "Notes on the Curse Formulae of the Tell Fekherye Inscription," *Revue biblique* 92 (1985): 54 (cf. Lev. 26:26). Although the order is different, Sefire I likewise warns, "Should seven nur[ses] anoint [. . . and] nurse a young boy, may he not have his fill; and should seven mares suckle a colt, may it not be sa[ted; and should seven] cows give suck to a calf, may it not have its fill; and should seven ewes suckle a lamb, [may it not be sa]ted." Joseph A. Fitzmyer, "The Aramaic Inscriptions of Sefire I and II," *Journal of the American Oriental Society* 81 (1961): 185. Deuteronomy 28:17–18 states in a similar, albeit more generic fashion, "Cursed be your basket and your kneading trough. Cursed be the fruit of your womb and the fruit of your land, the offspring of your cattle and the young of your flocks."

10. D. J. Wiseman, *The Vassal-Treaties of Esarhaddon* (London: British School of Archaeology in Iraq, 1958), 60, 78. See use of like language in Psalms 109:5 and 35:12 (cf. also 38:21), "They repay me evil for good."

11. Cf. Psalm 109:8, "May his days be few."

12. Cf. Deuteronomy 28:29, "You will be groping around at midday like a blind man gropes around in the darkness." Psalm 69:24 echoes, "May their eyes grow too dim to see." The curse of blindness was a common ancient Near Eastern curse motif, as, for example, in the Ugaritic tale of Aqhat, "May Baal make thee blind!" Pritchard, *ANET,* 155.

13. In Deuteronomy 28:26–35, the curses of war's carnage, skin diseases, blindness, rape, and pillaging prominently figure.

14. Cf. Deuteronomy 28:23, "The sky over your head will be bronze, and the ground beneath you iron," and the reverse imagery in Leviticus 26:19, "I will make your sky like iron and your ground like bronze."

15. Cf. Psalm 140:11, "Let burning coals fall upon them!" and the emended Psalm 11:6, "May he rain on the wicked coals of fire and brimstone."

16. Cf. the more extended treatment of the curse of familial cannibalism in Deuteronomy 28:53–57.

17. Cf. Psalm 109:18, "He wore cursing as his coat; so may it enter into his body like water, and into his bones like oil."

18. Wiseman, *Vassal-Treaties of Esarhaddon*, 60–78. The curse is seen to extend naturally to the family and descendents of the contracting party.

19. Fitzmyer, "Aramaic Inscriptions of Sefire I and II," 185.

20. Ibid. Such rites enhanced the effect of the pronounced curse, for the oath-taker would witness "what he calls down on himself should he be faithless." Dennis J. McCarthy, *Treaty and Covenant: A Study in Form in the Ancient Oriental Documents and in the Old Testament* (Rome: Biblical Institute Press, 1978), 149.

21. Ibid., 187. Although not strictly imprecatory, the concluding words of Revelation are reminiscent of the ancient inscriptional curses that accompa-

nied certain treaty documents. These gravely warn any who would tamper with its words: "If anyone should add to them, God will add to him the plagues described in this book. And if anyone should take away words from this book of prophecy, God will take away his share in the tree of life and in the holy city, which are described in this book" (Rev. 22:18–19).

22. "The *kudurru* was made to protect private property and especially the boundaries of property by extensive curse-formulae in the name of various gods. Any person who should damage the monument or cause the monument to be damaged, would inflict on himself all the curses of the inscription." F. Charles Fensham, "Common Trends in Curses of the Near Eastern Treaties and *Kudurru*-Inscriptions Compared with Maledictions of Amos and Isaiah," *Zeitschrift für die alttestamentliche Wissenschaft* 75 (1963): 158.

23. Timothy G. Crawford, *Blessing and Curse in Syro-Palestinian Inscriptions of the Iron Age,* American University Studies: Series 7, Theology and Religion (New York: Peter Lang, 1992), 120:97.

24. E.g., the funerary inscription of Sin-zer-ibni warns, "Whoever you are (who) shall remove this image and couch from its place, may ŠHR and ŠMŠ and NKL and NŠK tear out your name and *remainder* of life! And (with an evil) death may they kill you! And may they cause your seed to perish!" Gevirtz, "West-Semitic Curses," 148 (emphasis in original).

25. E.g., "This is (the tomb of Sheban)iah the royal steward. There is no silver or gold here, only (his bones) and the bones of his maidservant with him. Cursed be the man who opens this." John C. L. Gibson, *Textbook of Syrian Semitic Inscriptions,* vol. 1, *Hebrew and Moabite Inscriptions* (Oxford: Clarendon, 1971), 24.

26. Mercer, "Malediction in Cuneiform Inscriptions," 309.

27. Tzvi Abusch, "The Demonic Image of the Witch in Standard Babylonian Literature: The Reworking of Popular Conceptions by Learned Exorcists," in *Religion, Science, and Magic: In Concert and in Conflict,* ed. J. Neusner et al. (New York: Oxford University Press, 1989), 40.

28. Stanley Gevirtz, "Curse Motifs in the Old Testament and in the Ancient Near East" (Ph.D. diss., University of Chicago, 1959), 114.

29. Abusch, "Demonic Image of the Witch," 32–33. Notice the similarity of symptoms (and the locus of their cause in "baseless charges") between this series and the psalms of lament. But contrary to Mowinckel, the פֹּעֲלֵי אָוֶן, *po'ălêy 'āwen,* there do not designate those who "practice sorcery" but rather

those who "practice iniquity"—whether it be oppression, bloodshed, cursing, slander, or something else (cf. e.g., use in Pss. 14, 59, 64, 94, 141). Cf. Sigmund Mowinckel, *The Psalms in Israel's Worship,* trans. D. R. Ap-Thomas (Nashville: Abingdon, 1967), 2:3–7.

30. Cf. Psalm 7:17, "Let the trouble he has caused recoil on his head."

31. "Die Zauberin, die mich bezaubert hat: mit dem Zauber, mit dem sie mich bezaubert hat, bezaubere du sie!" Gerhard Meier, *Die assyrische Beschwörungssammlung Maqlû* (Berlin: Archiv für Orientforschung, Beiheft 2, 1937), 12.

32. Tzvi Abusch, "An Early Form of the Witchcraft Ritual *Maqlû* and the Origin of a Babylonian Magical Ceremony," in *Lingering over Words: Studies in Ancient Near Eastern Literature in Honor of William L. Moran,* ed. Tzvi Abusch et al., 1–57 (Atlanta: Scholars Press, 1990), 18.

33. Erica Reiner, *Šurpu: A Collection of Sumerian and Akkadian Incantations* (Graz: Archiv für Orientforschung, Beiheft 11, 1958), 2–3.

34. Ibid., 3.

35. Ibid., 30–31.

36. R. Campbell Thompson, *The Devils and Evil Spirits of Babylonia* (London: Luzac & Co., 1903; reprint, New York: AMS, 1976), 1:5, 7.

37. Sheldon H. Blank, "The Curse, Blasphemy, the Spell, and the Oath," *Hebrew Union College Annual* 23 (1950–51): 78 (emphasis in original).

38. Scharbert, "ארר," 1:416. Support for a magical understanding of the power of the curse in the ancient Near East has been further sought from the Hebrew Scriptures and the religion of early Israel. Two passages frequently claimed to show evidence of this magical view of the curse (and blessing) in the life of ancient Israel are Judges 17:1–2 and the account of Balaam in Numbers 22–24. In the former passage, it is relayed that Micah's mother had uttered a curse against a thief who had stolen from her a large sum of money. Upon her son's confession that he was the culprit, she immediately cries out, "Blessed be my son by Yahweh!" Blank believes this to be a forcible illustration of countermagic. A blessing is an effective antidote to a curse. Blank, "Curse, Blasphemy, the Spell, and the Oath," 94. Even if that supposition be granted, though—and it is far from certain—this passage by no means recounts orthodox Israelite theology, as the context makes clear. Verses 3 and following relate the relativism and idolatry characteristic of syncretism. There has always been in Israel's history the tendency toward

syncretism, and Yahweh has ever denounced it. Thus, if a proposition is to be legitimately established, it must be through genuine orthodoxy rather than perversions of Israelite religion. In the latter passage, the Moabite king, Balak, pleads a summons to Balaam: "Come now, curse for me this people. . . . For I know that whomever you bless are blessed, and whomever you curse are cursed" (Num. 22:6). It has been commonly inferred from this that Balaam possessed an unusual aptitude to produce, by mere utterance, profound effect for blessing or cursing. This may have been the pagan perception. The preponderance of evidence, however, identifies Balaam as a diviner (cf. Josh. 13:22; Num. 22:7) and further suggests that he belonged to a class of Akkadian diviners known as *bārû*, who were believed to accurately ascertain the will of the gods by means, typically, of the examination of the entrails or liver of a sacrificed animal. In this scenario, the desire of Balak is for Balaam, with his superior knowledge of his craft and record of success, to ascertain the divine will and also influence that will to his favor. Perhaps, then, the apparent power of Balaam's curse was reputed to be in his ability to "manipulate" the intent of the gods—something he found himself unable to even simulate with Yahweh. Moreover, since this account records a pagan king's perception of a pagan diviner's power to curse, repeatedly thwarted and overturned by Yahweh, it is more germane to the larger ancient Near Eastern understanding than to the understanding of ancient Israel.

39. Cf. Numbers 23:8, "How can I curse when God has not cursed?" and verse 20, "He has blessed, and I cannot change it."

40. See Deuteronomy 23:6, "However, Yahweh your God would not listen to Balaam, but Yahweh your God turned the curse into a blessing for you, because Yahweh your God loves you."

41. Yahweh admonished his priests in Malachi 2:2, "'If you do not listen, and if you do not set your heart to give honor to my name,' says Yahweh of Hosts, 'then I will send a curse upon you, and I will curse your blessings—indeed, I will curse them, because you have not so set your heart.'"

42. Herbert Chanan Brichto, *The Problem of "Curse" in the Hebrew Bible*, Journal of Biblical Literature Monograph Series (Philadelphia: Society of Biblical Literature, 1968),13:212.

43. Althann, "The Psalms of Vengeance Against Their Ancient Near Eastern Background," 4.

Chapter 3: Blood Bath: Psalm 58

1. Reading the defective spelling אֵלִם, ʾēlim (as in Exod. 15:11) contra MT's אֵלֶם, ʾēlem, "(in) silence."

2. יְתְמֹלָלוּ, yitmolālû, is literally, "thoroughly circumcised." By use of this metaphor, the psalmist may very well have been appealing for the "utter emasculation" of the judges' decrees of injustice.

3. Early and widespread uncertainty remains regarding the translation of this *hapax legomenon*. Given the prevalence of synonymous parallelism throughout this psalm, however, a similar construction is expected here.

4. Cf. Jesus' understanding of Psalm 82 in John 10:34–36, where his rebuttal to the Jews hinges on the identity of these "gods" as men—men who had received the word of God. Moreover, in the settings of Exodus 21:6; 22:8–9, 28 is some ambiguity in the use of the term (הָ)אֱלֹהִים, (hā) ʾĕlohîm—whether it refers to God or to his representatives who function judicially under his authority. This ambivalence is reinforced in Deuteronomy 19:17, where the two parties in dispute are called to "stand before Yahweh, before the priests and the judges."

5. Identity of these "gods" as leaders of the land, rather than "gods" of the heavenly court of Yahweh whose lackeys are the "wicked," is supported by a number of textual factors: (1) The crafted inclusion of verses 1 and 11 unifies the psalm; (2) the plausibly vocative "O sons of men" (cf. LXX, "O sons," οἱ υἱοί, *hoi huioi*) parallels "O gods" in verse 1; (3) mention of the "wicked" follows immediately and in a parallel thought that seems to equate the two groups; (4) the "wicked" are manifestly human—they are born and they bleed (vv. 3, 10); (5) the "gods" are confronted with a crime of speaking in verse 1, as are the "wicked" in verse 3 (perpetual deception); and (6) the "gods," if distinct from the "wicked," mysteriously disappear from the text and escape unscathed; but if they are equated with the "wicked," they receive due punishment. Regarding the latter four items, see David P. Wright, "Blown Away Like a Bramble: The Dynamics of Analogy in Psalm 58," *Revue biblique* 103 (1996): 219.

6. F. G. Hibbard, *The Psalms Chronologically Arranged, with Historical Introductions; and a General Introduction to the Whole Book,* 5th ed. (New York: Carlton & Porter, 1856), 120.

7. H. G. L. Peels, *The Vengeance of God: The Meaning of the Root NQM and the*

Function of the NQM-*Texts in the Context of Divine Revelation in the Old Testament,* Oudtestamentische Studiën, ed. A. S. Van der Woude (Leiden: E. J. Brill, 1995), 31:218.

8. John Piper, *"Love Your Enemies": Jesus' Love Command in the Synoptic Gospels and in the Early Christian Paraenesis* (Cambridge: Cambridge University Press, 1979), 117. Or, as Calvin dispassionately observes: "When righteousness is not rewarded, we are disposed to cherish unbelieving fears, and to imagine that God has retired from the government of the world, and is indifferent to its concerns." John Calvin, *Commentary on the Book of Psalms,* trans. J. Anderson (Edinburgh: Edinburgh Printing Co., 1846; reprint, Grand Rapids: Baker, 1979), 2:379.

9. Cf. Peels, *Vengeance of God,* 31:218.

10. Ibid., 31:214.

11. Jesus used a similarly strong "love/hate" dichotomy to emphasize the necessity of a disciple's "first loyalty" to him. Compare Matt. 10:37 with Luke 14:26.

12. Peels, *Vengeance of God,* 31:218. In this regard, see Psalm 68:21–23, which speaks in like language. Although envisioning an actual battle in which the foes of God are slain, it is also in some measure hyperbolic, to emphasize the sure and utter desolation of the wicked, that the righteous might exult in the triumph of God: "Surely God will smite the heads of his enemies, the hairy crowns of those who go on in their guilty ways. The Lord says, 'From Bashan I will bring them; I will bring them from the depths of the sea, that you may plunge your feet in blood, while the tongues of your dogs have their share of your foes.'"

13. Derek Kidner, *Psalms 1–72,* Tyndale Old Testament Commentaries, ed. D. J. Wiseman (London: Inter-Varsity, 1973), 27.

14. Kraus comments regarding the thrust of this psalm: "It is when injustice has become intolerable that the plea for God's intervention resounds." Hans-Joachim Kraus, *Psalms 1–59: A Commentary,* trans. Hilton C. Oswald (Minneapolis: Augsburg, 1988), 537.

15. Erich Zenger, *A God of Vengeance? Understanding the Psalms of Divine Wrath,* trans. L. M. Maloney (Louisville: Westminster John Knox, 1996), 38.

16. Calvin, *Commentary on the Book of Psalms,* 2:378.

17. Ibid., 4:283.

18. James 5:1–6 speaks in like caustic manner against the rich who, for their

own gain, had exploited their workers and manipulated the court system to condemn the innocent:

> [1]Listen now, you rich, weep and howl at your coming miseries! [2]Your wealth has rotted and your clothes have become moth-eaten. [3]Your gold and silver have corroded, and their tarnish will be a testimony against you and will eat your flesh like fire. You have hoarded treasure in the last days. [4]Look! The wages you withheld from the workers who mowed your fields cries out against you, and the cries of the harvesters have entered the ears of the Lord of Hosts. [5]You have lived on earth in luxury and self-indulgence; you have nourished your hearts in the day of slaughter; [6]you have condemned and murdered the righteous, who did not oppose you.

This pronouncement of both present woe and impending doom is then juxtaposed to an encouragement for the righteous to endure patiently such injustice, based upon the assurance that the coming of the Lord is near, and he will judge (vv. 7–11). Although not identical to the character of the imprecatory psalms, verses 1–11 above betray a similar ethic: sometimes the righteous should cry out for God to judge severe or violent oppressors, even as they remain steadfast in suffering, leaving justice to the divine Judge. The veiled reference to the "cries of the harvesters entering the ears of the Lord of Hosts" (v. 4) is notable in this regard. Such cries for justice were voiced in the imprecatory psalms. Indeed, Adamson calls Psalm 58 "a striking parallel" to this passage. James B. Adamson, *The Epistle of James*, New International Commentary on the New Testament, ed. F. F. Bruce (Grand Rapids: Eerdmans, 1979), 184. Series hereafter cited as NICNT. James 5:10, gives the Old Testament prophets as examples of patience under unjust suffering. These same prophets sometimes uttered maledictions against hardened and injurious enemies (e.g., Jer. 18:18–23, which uses words strikingly reminiscent of Ps. 109), even though they were characterized by their "long-suffering" or "slow temper" (μακροθυμία, *makrothymia*).

19. Dietrich Bonhoeffer, "A Bonhoeffer Sermon," trans. D. Bloesch, ed. F. B. Nelson, *Theology Today* 38 (1982): 469.

20. James E. Adams, *War Psalms of the Prince of Peace: Lessons from the Imprecatory Psalms* (Phillipsburg, N.J.: Presbyterian & Reformed, 1991), 103.

21. Cf. Psalms 58:10–11; 79:9–10; 94:1–2, in which the expectation of divine vengeance forms the backdrop for the psalmists' cries.

22. Peter Craigie comments, "The song was not only a song of witness for the present, but one that would continue to be sung in the future, thus bearing a continuing witness of the covenant commitment and reminding the people of the implications of a breach of the covenant." Peter C. Craigie, *The Book of Deuteronomy*, New International Commentary on the Old Testament, ed. R. K. Harrison (Grand Rapids: Eerdmans, 1976), 374. Series hereafter cited as NICOT.

23. S. R. Driver remarks that "the thought underlying the whole is thus the rescue of the people, by an act of grace, at the moment when annihilation seemed imminent. The poem begins reproachfully; but, in general, tenderness and pity prevail above severity, and towards the close the strain rises into one of positive encouragement and promise." S. R. Driver, *A Critical and Exegetical Commentary on Deuteronomy*, International Critical Commentary on the Holy Scriptures of the Old and New Testaments, ed. Samuel Rolles Driver et al., 3d ed. (n.p., 1902; reprint, Edinburgh: T. & T. Clark, 1965), 344.

24. Although the text is notoriously ambiguous, it is contextually most likely that the referents to "them" and "their" switch at verse 31 from rebellious Israel to her pagan oppressors ("for *their* rock is not like *our* Rock," emphasis added), and then back to Israel at verse 36 ("Yahweh will judge/vindicate his people").

25. Or "vindicate." Although the primary nuance of דִּין (*dîn*) in this passage is that of "vindication" (cf. the immediate parallelism and the focal element in vv. 41–43), there is a certain purposeful contextual ambiguity, embracing the nuance of "judgment," based upon the presence of God's enemies even among God's people (cf. vv. 36–38). Yahweh will principally punish the heathen who oppress Israel, but he also will punish the wicked in Israel who oppress the righteous. C. F. Keil and F. Delitzsch, *The Pentateuch*, Biblical Commentary on the Old Testament, trans. J. Martin (Edinburgh: T.&T. Clark, 1866; reprint, Grand Rapids: Eerdmans, 1963), 3:487–88. This secondary sense is shown in Psalm 50:4 (cf. v. 16ff.), which borrows the language of Deuteronomy 32:1, 36: "He calls to the heavens above, and to the earth, *to judge his people* (לָדִין עַמּוֹ, *lādîn ʿammô*, emphasis added)."

26. This additional line has been adopted, following principally the testimony

of Qumran (4QDeut^Q), supported in large measure by the LXX. The resulting five cola structure of verse 43 parallels that of verse 39. Both are climactic in form and pivotal in theology.

27. In Deuteronomy 32, the enemies who suffer the vengeance of God are ostensibly heathen oppressors; Psalm 58 uses the language and tone, expanding it to include ungodly oppressors in general—even if they are among God's own people (cf. similar usage and expansion in Isa. 1).

28. The psalmist borrows Deuteronomy's imagery of poisonous snakes, using it metaphorically, as does the Song of Moses (cf. the literal image in Deut. 32:24 with the manifestly metaphorical use in verse 33).

29. "The prophets stressed 'the day of the Lord's vengeance' (Isa. 38:8; 61:2; 63:4) as times in history when the Lord sets the record straight. This was Jeremiah's view of the fall of Jerusalem. Since in the course of history the record can never be totally straight the prophetic *eschaton* or final day of the Lord's vengeance is called for." Elmer B. Smick, "נָקַם," *TWOT*, 2:599.

30. There is vigorous debate as to the text identified in Revelation 15 as "the Song of Moses." By literary tie and thematic reference, it is likely that both Deuteronomy 32 and Exodus 15 are meant, although Deuteronomy 32 bears the *primary* emphasis: (1) Deuteronomy 32 usually is known as "the Song of Moses"; (2) There is a distinct allusion to Deuteronomy 32:4 in Revelation 15:3 ("just and true," cf. 16:7); (3) More conclusively, although some reference to the Song of the Sea may be present (Exod. 15), and although the plagues in Revelation 16 bear a striking resemblance to the plagues against Egypt as the prelude to the Exodus, the principal issue of Revelation in context is the cry for and coming of divine vengeance. Note vengeance as the central issue of the latter portion of the "Song" in Deuteronomy 32, but not of Exodus 15, the anticipation of vengeance in Revelation 6, and the fulfillment in 15–19 (cf., e.g., the reference in Rev. 16:6 to requiting the shed blood of the saints, with Deut. 32:43). This connection takes on added meaning as Revelation binds the Song of Moses to that of the Lamb. As the book progresses to its climax, it is the Lamb slain who returns as Avenger (cf. Rev. 5 and 19).

31. The covenant lawsuit pattern (רִיב, *rîb*) is the central form in Deuteronomy 32. But this Song is, as Wright recognizes, "a 'broken' *rîb*, that is, a specific cultic form adapted and expanded by other themes to serve a more generalized purpose in confession and praise." G. Ernest Wright, "The Lawsuit of

God: A Form-Critical Study of Deuteronomy 32," in *Israel's Prophetic Heritage: Essays in Honor of James Muilenburg*, ed. B. W. Anderson, W. Harrelson (New York: Harper & Brothers, 1962), 40–41.

32. One may listen to how the Song of Moses—particularly the refrain, "It is mine to avenge, I will repay" (Deut. 32:35)—lilts its way through the pages of Scripture. It is the basis of many imprecations in the Psalms, the foundation of New Testament ethics in Romans 12:19, and a song of triumph in Revelation 15:3–4; 19:1–2 (in response to 6:9–11).

Chapter 4: Baby Bashing: Psalm 137

1. The lack of an explicit object here (frequently supplied in translations) has led to several conjectures that would lead to a translation, "May my right hand wither/fail." In contrast, however, the theme of "remembering" (Ps. 137:6–7) and "forgetting" (v. 5) pervasive in the surrounding verses of this psalm lends weight to the MT as it stands, with the expected meaning "to forget," with poetic ellipsis. The elided object is probably "its skill" or some such equivalent, as is frequently supplied in translations, since it is likely that the psalmist here was a temple musician (cf. vv. 2–6). The self-imposed curse was thus placed upon those faculties most pertinent to his vocation.

2. The reference to the cliff (הַסֶּלַע, *hassālaʿ*) seems at first incongruous when juxtaposed with judgment upon Babylon, for, as Howard Osgood notes, "Babylonia is a perfectly flat alluvial country where no hill, nor stone, nor rock, nor cliff is to be found." Osgood interprets the description as a "metaphor of Babylon's being hurled from her exaltation in pride and power, for the literal interpretation is ridiculous." Howard Osgood, "Dashing the Little Ones Against the Rock," *Princeton Theological Review* 1 (1903): 35. The terminology was probably chosen, however, not because of its geographical precision, but because of its known association with Edom (Obad. 3) and Babylon in prophetic judgment oracles. In Jeremiah 51:25, God promises to roll Babylon off "the cliffs," (הַסְּלָעִים, *hassĕlāʿîm*). The imagery had become somewhat stereotypical for utter destruction in judgment. Moreover, such language may have been used intentionally to remind of something experienced by the Judeans at the hands of the Babylonians. In addition, although סֶלַע (*selaʿ*) more commonly refers to a cliff or sharp crag, it is also used of the broad, bare foundation rock of the soon-to-be-leveled city of

Tyre in Ezekiel 26:4, 14. This shows that a relatively broad range of meaning included a definition applicable here.

3. Erich Zenger, *A God of Vengeance? Understanding the Psalms of Divine Wrath,* trans. L. M. Maloney (Louisville: Westminster John Knox, 1996), 46.

4. R. E. O. White, *A Christian Handbook to the Psalms* (Grand Rapids: Eerdmans, 1984), 200.

5. Artur Weiser, *The Psalms,* trans. H. Hartwell, Old Testament Library, ed. G. E. Wright et al. (Philadelphia: Westminster, 1962), 796.

6. As Derek Kidner argues, "To cut this witness out of the Old Testament would be to impair its value as revelation." Derek Kidner, *Psalms 73–150,* Tyndale Old Testament Commentaries, ed. D. J. Wiseman (London: Inter-Varsity, 1975), 461. He believes, however, that the revelatory value of these verses is localized principally in disclosing the sinfulness of man and the necessity of the Cross.

7. John Bright, *The Authority of the Old Testament* (Nashville: Abingdon, 1967), 238.

8. C. S. Lewis, *Reflections on the Psalms* (New York: Harcourt, Brace & Co., 1958), 136. Fifteen centuries earlier, Augustine of Hippo, in his commentary on the Psalms, likewise asked, "What are the little ones of Babylon? Evil desires at their birth. For there are, who have to fight with inveterate lusts. When lust is born, before evil habit giveth it strength against thee, when lust is little, by no means let it gain the strength of evil habit; when it is little, dash it. But thou fearest, lest though dashed it die not; 'Dash it against the Rock; and that Rock is Christ.'" Augustin, *Saint Augustin: Expositions on the Book of Psalms,* ed. A. C. Coxe, A Select Library of the Nicene and Post-Nicene Fathers of the Christian Church, ed. P. Schaff, trans. J. E. Tweed et al. (New York: Charles Scribner's Sons, 1917), 8:632.

9. Cf. Osgood, "Dashing the Little Ones Against the Rock," 35–37.

10. Cf. the horrors promised by God in the curses of Deuteronomy 28:53–57. Also, the Assyrian king Sennacherib speaks in his annals of besieging several cities, one of which was Ekron: "I assaulted Ekron and killed the officials and patricians who had committed the crime and hung their bodies on poles surrounding the city." James B. Pritchard, ed., *Ancient Near Eastern Texts Relating to the Old Testament,* 3d ed. with supplement (Princeton, N.J.: Princeton University Press, 1969), 288.

11. Ibid., 539–40.

12. The Scriptures document this practice as committed against Israel in 2 Kings 8:9–12 and Amos 1:13. Even Israel learned to practice these savage ways (2 Kings 15:14, 16).

13. Leslie C. Allen, *Psalms 101–150,* Word Biblical Commentary, ed. D. A. Hubbard and G. W. Barker (Waco, Tex.: Word, 1983), 21:237. Such an act serves as a macabre illustration of the depth of human depravity when the restraining hand of God is removed. Sin always destroys mercilessly.

14. Alfred Guillaume, "The Meaning of תולל in Psalm 137 [3]," *Journal of Biblical Literature* 75 (1956): 144.

15. Zenger, *A God of Vengeance?* 47.

16. Bobby J. Gilbert, "An Exegetical and Theological Study of Psalm 137" (Th.M. thesis, Dallas Theological Seminary, 1981), 75.

17. Although implicit in the veiled imprecations of verses 8–9, such an appeal and surrender of vengeance is made explicit in verse 7.

18. Gordon J. Wenham, *The Book of Leviticus,* NICOT (Grand Rapids: Eerdmans, 1979), 312. This principle of just recompense, embodied in the *lex talionis,* forms the foundation in any period for any civilized judicial system.

19. John Wenham agrees that it is "a misunderstanding of the Sermon on the Mount to imagine that our Lord is repudiating the principle of civil justice, or undercutting the authority of the Old Testament." Rather, "the whole passage is concerned with misinterpretations of the Old Testament, not with any supposedly sub-standard regulations. The *lex talionis* . . . was being used as an instrument of personal revenge. Our Lord says that the citizen of the kingdom is to have an utter disregard for his own rights. . . . He must love his enemies and harbour no desire for vengeance in his heart. That is a very different matter from telling a judge not to administer justice." John W. Wenham, *The Goodness of God* (Downers Grove, Ill.: InterVarsity, 1974), 94–95.

20. Gilbert, "Exegetical and Theological Study of Psalm 137," 69 (emphasis in original).

21. Cf. this trans-testamental law to its sibling "law of sowing and reaping" (Prov. 26:27; Hos. 8:7; 10:12–13; Gal. 6:7–8) and our Lord's own version: "With the measure you use it will be measured to you" (Matt. 7:2).

22. That the commands of the old order find their climax in Christ does not mean that the principles underlying these commands—particularly those that unmistakably express the character of God—are categorically done away with. Rather, if a divine command issued to the nation of Israel clearly

reflected the justice of God, then the underlying principle remains—for the use and benefit of the New Testament church.

23. From the roots שדד (*šdd*), שלם (*šlm*), and גמל (*gml*), respectively.

24. Cf. Kidner, *Psalms 73–150,* 460.

25. Note Jeremiah 50:15, 28–29; 51:6, 11, 24, 35–36, 49, 56. This violent vengeance to be enacted against deserving Babylon is by the word of Yahweh, so there is an essential "rightness" to it.

26. Note also reference to the "day" of Babylon's judgment (cf. Jer. 50:27, 31; 51:2; Deut. 32:35), and the divinely uttered oath (cf. Jer. 51:14; Deut. 32:40–41).

27. Psalm 79:12 cries out, "Pay back into the laps of our neighbors *seven times* the reproach they have hurled at you, O Lord!" (emphasis added). This appears on the surface to be a savage appeal to super-retaliation, and has been named "an echo of the viciousness of Lamech (Gen. 4:24)." Walter Brueggemann, *The Message of the Psalms: A Theological Commentary* (Minneapolis: Augsburg, 1984), 72. This plea for sevenfold recompense, however, is an image borrowed from the lips of Yahweh himself. In Genesis 4:15, Yahweh promises the murderer Cain that anyone who killed him would himself receive "seven times" vengeance. More germane to the context of Psalm 79, in Leviticus 26 Yahweh repeatedly promises sevenfold punishment for stubborn covenant breaking (Lev. 26:18, 21, 24, 28). Whether this sevenfold *lex talionis* is to be construed as (1) a figure for sure and full punishment (preferably), (2) literary convention (hyperbole), or (3) starkly literal, it must be questioned carefully, for the psalmist is harking back to language initiated by Yahweh himself and uttered for the highest cause: the sake of his honor.

28. C. H. Spurgeon, *The Treasury of David: Psalms 125–150* (New York: Funk and Wagnalls, 1886), 7:189.

29. Cf. Jeremiah 51:48, "Then they will shout for joy over Babylon—heaven and earth and all that is in them."

30. One of William Webb's chief objections to this psalm in particular, and to the imprecatory psalms in general, is this very specificity. His contention is that such appeals from a Christian perspective, in moving toward an ultimate ethic, would be transmuted into more general cries for justice, with the specifics of that justice left out of the prayer itself and completely in God's control. William J. Webb, "Bashing Babies Against the Rocks: A Redemptive-Movement Approach to the Imprecatory Psalms" (Evangelical Theological Society Paper, November 2003).

31. There are certain passages in the New Testament that unmistakably echo the essence of the *lex talionis*. Paul's curse of Elymas the sorcerer, for example, found in Acts 13:6–12, derives from this principle: Elymas had sought to keep the proconsul in spiritual blindness, so he was cursed with physical blindness. Likewise, Paul's confidence regarding the antagonistic Alexander (2 Tim. 4:14) is clearly based upon the *lex talionis*. And perhaps most notable in its conspicuous commendation of this law is Revelation 18. The principle of the *lex talionis* is the theme that pervades the passage, and at its divine enactment against eschatological Babylon, an attitude of rejoicing is exacted from both saint and angel alike (Rev. 18:20).

32. Allen, *Psalms 101–150*, 21:242.

33. Gilbert, "Exegetical and Theological Study of Psalm 137," 83.

Chapter 5: Unholy Litany: Psalm 109

1. Thus, this psalm was intended for temple worship. This has led some to conclude that the frightening curses of verses 6–19 must be the recollection of curses *against* David by his enemies rather than the curses of David himself. By the example of other psalms, however (e.g., notably Ps. 88), much more was appropriately brought before God in community worship than current sensibilities generally allow.

2. Translating interpretively, as suited to the context. The frugal Hebrew is literally, "but I, a prayer,"—i.e., "I am characterized by prayer/a man of prayer" (cf. Ps. 120:7, אֲנִי־שָׁלוֹם, *'ănî-šālôm*).

3. The setting envisaged is that of a courtroom, in which David desires his oppressor to stand trial for his crimes before a harsh prosecutor and merciless judge, in accord with the harshness and lack of mercy the enemy displayed. David seeks a verdict of "guilty." For certain parallels with the imagery of this psalm, see Zechariah 3.

4. Calvin translates verse 17 similarly, with jussive (commanding) intent: "As he loved cursing, so let it come upon him: as he did not take delight in blessing, so let it be far from him." Calvin, *Commentary on the Book of Psalms*, trans. J. Anderson (Edinburgh: Edinburgh Printing Company, 1847), 4:283. He further explains that, although the words are in the past tense (in the MT), "it is necessary to translate them as expressive of a wish or desire; for David continues to pray that his enemy may be visited with the same

unparalleled ills which he had inflicted upon others" (cf. 109:16). Ibid., 284. Various English versions likewise translate this and the following verses as bearing a jussive nuance.

5. Literally, "This, the payment of my accusers from Yahweh." This verbless phrase continues the jussive appeal of verse 19 yet also appears to embody all the curses of the preceding verses as a prelude to the climactic "but you . . ." (v. 21).

6. The appeal to Yahweh's "name" is an appeal to his character, especially his inestimable "loving-kindness," as evidenced by the parallel phrase.

7. Joseph Hammond, "An Apology for the Vindictive Psalm (Psalm cix)," *Expositor* 2 (1875): 325.

8. Ragnar C. Teigen, "Can Anything Good Come from a Curse?" *Lutheran Quarterly* 26 (1974): 49.

9. Walter Brueggemann, *The Message of the Psalms: A Theological Commentary* (Minneapolis: Augsburg, 1984), 83.

10. C. S. Lewis, *Christian Reflections,* ed. W. Hooper (Grand Rapids: Eerdmans, 1967), 118. And he adds that the psalmist "was doubtless a hot-blooded barbarian."

11. C. H. Spurgeon, *The Treasury of David: Psalms 104–118* (New York: Funk and Wagnalls, 1881), 5:157.

12. D. J. Wiseman, *The Vassal-Treaties of Esarhaddon* (London: British School of Archaeology in Iraq, 1958), 60. Cf. also Psalm 109:18, "He wore cursing as his coat; so may it enter into his body like water and into his bones like oil," with Esarhaddon's, "[As oil en]ters your flesh, [just so may] they cause this curse to enter into your flesh." Ibid., 78.

13. Calvin, *Commentary on the Book of Psalms,* 4:276.

14. Arguments can be cited for this view. Some of the chief are as follows: (1) The Psalms sometimes use unattributed quotations—whether brief (e.g., Pss. 22:9; 137:3) or lengthy (e.g., Ps. 50:7–15). (2) Whereas verses 6–19 castigate the enemy in the singular, the verses that precede and follow present the enemy in the plural. Artur Weiser asserts that the change to the singular in vv. 6–19 is accounted for only if vv. 6–19 quote the imprecations that had been directed against the psalmist. Artur Weiser, *The Psalms,* trans. H. Hartwell, Old Testament Library, ed. G. E. Wright et al. (Philadelphia: Westminster, 1962), 691. (3) The structure of verse 20, in particular, is atypical and thus internally highlighted. Its verbless construction differs from the verses preceding, where

jussives prevail. It is introduced by the emphatic "this!" (זֹאת, *zô³t*). This verse is juxtaposed to "but you" (וְאַתָּה, *wĕ³attāh*) at the beginning of verse 21, which indicates that a change has taken place. As Hans-Joachim Kraus argues, after the petitioner in the previous verses has revealed the enemy's curses to Yahweh, he turns to Yahweh. Hans-Joachim Kraus, *Psalms 60–150*, trans. H. C. Oswald (Minneapolis: Augsburg, 1989), 338. (4) Verses 6–19 appear to be set in a framework of repeated terms. Of particular note are *evil* (109:5, 20); "speaking" terms (109:2–3, 20); the repeated verb *to accuse* (109:4, 20). Leslie C. Allen asks, "Is not this repetition the psalmist's own signal that first he is about to quote the words of accusation and then has finished quoting them?" Leslie C. Allen, *Psalms 101–150*, Word Biblical Commentary, ed. D. A. Hubbard and G. W. Barker (Waco, Tex.: Word, 1983), 21:73.

The difficulties with this view, however, outweigh the apparent support: (1) Whereas the use of non-explicitly introduced quotations is common in the Psalms, they are in general contextually quite clear and readily recognized. This is not the case with Psalm 109. (2) Switching between plural and singular is not unknown to the Psalms. Notably, in Psalm 55, David uses such a change to set out the central element of enmity against him—a friend turned traitor. The same may be at work in Psalm 109. (3) The effect of verse 20, as introduced by the stark and abrupt *this!* may be to gather all the foregoing curses in a fist and deliver them in a single pugilistic punch. This would be the forceful prelude to the climactic and structurally disjunctive *but you* of verse 21. David P. Wright, "Ritual Analogy in Psalm 109," *Journal of Biblical Literature* 113 (1994): 400. (4) The verbal inclusions may simply be a literary device or a means of giving "complete contextual justification for a curse by the psalmist in vv. 6–19." Wright, "Ritual Analogy in Psalm 109," 394. Besides the repetitions observed by Allen, note the repeated designation *poor and needy* (vv. 16, 22), the term *judge/condemn* (vv. 7, 31), and the placement of an accuser versus the presence of Yahweh at the "right hand" (vv. 6, 31). These instances do not frame verses 6–19 and call into question Allen's assertion.

Also, it is plausible that there is further imprecation in verses 28b–29 in less vitriolic language. If so, and verses 6–19 are in essence ignoble, how is it to be satisfactorily interpreted? The exclamations of verses 16–18 (e.g., "he loved cursing") are certainly not true of David; even his enemies would not label this man in such language. The description does fit some of his enemies (e.g., Shimei—2 Sam. 16:5–13). Also, in various other psalms, David unquestionably makes a cry of imprecation against his enemies (e.g., Pss. 35:4–8; 58:6–9; 69:23–29). The quotation hypothesis does not, in fact, remove the essential moral difficulty—to say nothing of other scathing imprecations in Scripture. Most of these have been left in the canon without divine disparagement or condemnation.

15. Peter relates that it was the Holy Spirit who spoke these things through David (Acts 1:16).

16. Spurgeon comments,

> We could all pray for the conversion of our worst enemy, and David would have done the same; but viewing the adversaries of the Lord, and doers of iniquity, AS SUCH, AND AS INCORRIGIBLE we cannot wish them well; on the contrary, we desire their overthrow, and destruction. The gentlest hearts burn with indignation when they hear of barbarities to women and children, of crafty plots for ruining the innocent, of cruel oppression of helpless orphans, and gratuitous ingratitude to the good and gentle. A curse upon the perpetrators of the atrocities in Turkey may not be less virtuous than a blessing upon the righteous. (Spurgeon, *The Treasury of David*, 5:157)

17. This thread of "loving-kindness" (חֶסֶד, *ḥesed*) weaves its way through the psalm. David appeals for the withholding of loving-kindness from the enemy (109:12) because the enemy had himself habitually withheld it from those who desperately needed it (v. 16). David twice appeals to Yahweh's loving-kindness as the basis for deliverance from his plight (vv. 21, 26).

18. Psalm 109 utilizes the language and imagery of the court: accusation and condemnation (both wrongful and just), along with prosecution and defense (vv. 2–4, 6–7, 31).

19. David speaks as the innocent sufferer, in the language of the judicial court and in accord with the standard of justice and punishment it must uphold.

20. Other imprecatory Davidic psalms identify known personal enemies. Psalm 54:7 concerns the Ziphites, 56:8 the Philistines and other enemies, and 59:6, 12–14 are uttered against the men of Saul sent to kill him.

21. As such, it is not a psalm to be relegated to the partially revealed religion or supposed "inferior ethics" of the Old Testament—for the ethics of both

testaments are in essence the same, and the revelation of both proceeds from the same God, who does not change. Nor can the demand be solely explained by the Old Testament's focus on the outworking of divine justice in the temporal sphere while the Christian awaits the eschatological Day. In the Scriptures, the demand is but a matter both of emphasis and the progress of revelation. The Old Testament holds forth in germinal form the same hope of eschatological judgment as the New (e.g., Isa. 66:22–24). The New Testament assumes the same expectation of temporal justice as the Old (e.g., Rom. 1:18–32; 13:3–4).

22. As such, it is an expression of the psalmist's confidence in divine action on his behalf.

23. The imprecatory psalms base their theology of cursing in the Torah, the foundational revelation of God. Although the psalmist here does not quote from Genesis 12:3 *per se,* he evidently invokes the theology classically expressed there—the divine promise to curse those who curse his people. This promise of divine blessing and cursing was to operate at both individual and corporate levels: the promise was given to Abram and yet applied to all his descendents—all who would enter that covenant by faith. Later allusions to this promise were likewise applied both individually and corporately. For the former sense, cf. Genesis 27:29, in the blessing of Jacob by Isaac—acquired by deception, yet binding nonetheless: "Cursed be those who curse you, and blessed be those who bless you." For the latter, cf. Numbers 24:9, from the lips of Balaam, hired by Balak to curse the encroaching nation of Israel but frustrated by the will of Yahweh to bless instead: "Blessed be those who bless you, and cursed be those who curse you" (cf. also Exod. 23:22; Deut. 30:7). This dual application seems to run through the prophets. See the personal imprecations in Jeremiah 18:18–23; the judgments against various surrounding nations for their sins against Israel, along with (notably) judgments against Israel for harming their own people (specifically the righteous and the needy) in Amos 1–2; and the judgments promised against Edom in Obadiah 8–15.

24. Both אָרַר (*ʾārar*) and קִלֵּל (*qillēl*) mean "to curse," although the former is characteristically solemn and judicial (e.g., Deut. 27:15–26), whereas the latter often bears the nuance "to disdain" (e.g., Exod. 21:17). Thus, Genesis 12:3 says that "those who in the future would view Abraham and all that his faith and life represented as contemptible would find that they would come under

God's judicial curse. To curse Abraham would be almost equivalent to cursing God." Allan M. Harman, "The Continuity of the Covenant Curses in the Imprecations of the Psalter," *Reformed Theological Review* 54 (1995): 68.

25. J. Carl Laney recognizes that the cries for judgment in the imprecatory psalms relate to provisions of the Abrahamic covenant. He contends, however, that they "are appeals for Yahweh to carry out His judgment against those who would curse *the nation*." J. Carl Laney, "A Fresh Look at the Imprecatory Psalms," *Bibliotheca Sacra* 138 (1981): 42 (emphasis added).

26. Faith dominates the foundational narrative of Genesis 12–22. See also the examples of non-Israelites incorporated into the covenant community of faith and the promises to Abraham (e.g., Rahab the Canaanite and Ruth the Moabite: Josh. 6:25; Ruth 1:16; 4:13–22; Matt. 1:5).

27. This theme is common to ancient Near Eastern suzerain-vassal treaties. E.g., the Hittite treaty between Mursilis and Duppi-Tessub of Amurru includes the prescription, "With my friend you shall be friend, and with my enemy you shall be enemy." James B. Pritchard, ed., *Ancient Near Eastern Texts Relating to the Old Testament*, 3d ed. with supplement (Princeton, N.J.: Princeton University Press, 1969), 204. Likewise, in the covenant between Yahweh and his people, he promised upon their obedience, "I will be an enemy to your enemies, and I will be a foe to your foes" (Exod. 23:22).

28. And yet (as revealed in these texts) his justice, although harsh, pales in comparison to his loving-kindness.

29. H. G. L. Peels, *The Vengeance of God: The Meaning of the Root NQM and the Function of the NQM-Texts in the Context of Divine Revelation in the Old Testament*, Oudtestamentische Studiën, ed. A. S. Van der Woude (Leiden: E. J. Brill, 1995), 31:240.

30. As Paul proclaims in Galatians 3:8, the "gospel" we share with Abraham is the promise that "in you all nations will be blessed" (Gen. 12:3b). This portion of the Abrahamic promise is immediately preceded by the consolation that "I will bless those who bless you, and he who curses you I will curse" (Gen. 12:3a).

31. See the Parable of the Sheep and the Goats (Matt. 25:31–46) and the post-Cross example of Paul and Barnabas (Acts 13:51).

32. John Wenham comments that this display "is a symbolic act of solemn cursing," and further notes that "the disciples' curse is a most solemn warning of the day of judgment." John W. Wenham, *The Goodness of God* (Downers

Grove, Ill.: InterVarsity, 1974), 157. This illustrates that in the Scriptures there is often a measure of "blending" (semantic interplay and functional overlap) between the categories of "curse" and "announcement of judgment, warning, or woe." Context informs the intent.

33. A significant number of early Christians did understand Paul's statement in an imprecatory sense. Although undoubtedly a secondary reading, the Byzantine tradition (along with a portion of the Western) explicitly transmitted this imprecatory intent through the optative ἀποδώῃ (*apodōē*). Also, as Paul directly continues, we see modeled differing appropriate responses to enmity. To the hardened and harmful, Paul issues this sobering sentence, but to those who wronged him out of fear, deserting him in his desperate need, he pleads, "May it not be counted against them" (2 Tim. 4:16).

34. Brueggemann, *Message of the Psalms,* 87.

35. Erich Zenger, *A God of Vengeance? Understanding the Psalms of Divine Wrath,* trans. L. M. Maloney (Louisville: Westminster John Knox, 1996), 92 (emphasis in original).

Chapter 6: Apparent Contradictions

1. The Sermon on the Mount is specifically introduced as given to "his disciples" (Matt. 5:1–2).

2. Cf. Luke 24:27, 44–45; John 5:39–40, 46. For those who have seen Christ, the Old Testament will never be the same.

3. D. A. Carson, *The Sermon on the Mount: An Evangelical Exposition of Matthew 5–7* (Grand Rapids: Baker, 1978), 37 (emphasis in original).

4. Jesus used hyperbole for the sake of startling emphasis. Cf., e.g., the parallel utterances of Christ in Matthew 10:37 and Luke 14:26. Luke states in stark hyperbole, "If anyone comes to me and does not *hate* his father and mother . . . he cannot be my disciple." Matthew softens the same idea to comparison: "He who *loves* father or mother *more than* me is not worthy of me" (emphasis added).

5. This call for perfection serves as a reminder that the demands of God are impossible apart from divine enabling and may be truly obeyed only by relying on God and his grace.

6. In the full pericope of Matthew 5:43–48, verse 48 carries the dual function of summing up both the premier and overarching command to love, as

well as the larger preceding pericope of 5:20–48, tying our activity to the prior activity of God, who is our exemplar. Verses 46–47 illustrate the command of enemy-love in tangible form.

7. These words are paralleled in Luke 6:27–28, 35–36:

> Love your enemies, do good to those who hate you, bless those who curse you, pray for those who mistreat you. . . . But love your enemies and do good to them and lend to them, expecting nothing in return. Then your reward will be great, and you will be sons of the Most High, because he is kind to the ungrateful and evil. Be compassionate, just as also your Father is compassionate.

8. Some argue that the command to hate your enemy is a fair summary of the Old Testament's instruction in this matter. Against this view, E. F. Sutcliffe summarizes what the men of Qumran would have learned from the Old Testament with regard to God's and the believer's attitude toward the enemy:

> God hates sin and sinners too, precisely in so far as they are attached to sin, because as sinful they attract to themselves the hatred due to sin. Nonetheless God desires their repentance and longs to forgive. But if they persist in the stubbornness of their evil wills, He is obliged in justice to punish and to avenge. So too the pious Israelite, following the ways of God, hates sin and sinners and is called upon at times to act as the instrument of divine vengeance. But he must not entertain any personal hate or rancor. On the contrary he must act kindly even to those hostile to himself. He is commanded to love his neighbor as himself and this commandment embraces also foreigners resident in the land. He must act in regard of all even as he would wish others to act in regard of himself. (E. F. Sutcliffe, "Hatred at Qumran," *Revue de Qumran* 2 [1960]: 349).

9. James H. Charlesworth, ed., *The Dead Sea Scrolls: Hebrew, Aramaic, and Greek Texts with English Translations,* vol. 1, *Rule of the Community and Related Documents* (Louisville: Westminster John Knox, 1994), 6–7.

10. "But I will have no compassion for any who rebel against the way." Ibid., 46–47.

11. This mind-set was not isolated solely to the Qumran sectarians, for the general populace held a hatred toward Samaritans in general and in principle (cf. Neh. 4; 6; John 4:9). The Zealots felt such rancor against the Romans that the zealots' very existence was sustained by the violent objective to overthrow and expel Rome and its influence from their land.

12. These words are the antithesis of both Jesus' words in Matthew 5 and the apostle Paul's in Romans 12.

13. Bruce M. Metzger, ed., *The Oxford Annotated Apocrypha, Revised Standard Version,* expanded ed. (Oxford: Oxford University Press, Inc., 1977), 143. Contrast this advice with that of the ancient pagan Babylonian *Counsels of Wisdom* (1700–1600 B.C.):

> Do not return evil to the man who disputes with you;
> Requite with kindness your evildoer,
> Maintain justice to your enemy,
> Smile on your adversary.
> If your ill-wisher is [. . . ,] nurture him.
> Do not set your [mind] on evil.
> . . . [. . .] agreeable [to] the gods.
> Evil [. . .] an abomination [. . . of] Marduk.
> . . . .
> Give food to eat, beer to drink,
> Grant what is asked, provide for and honour.
> In this a man's god takes pleasure,
> It is pleasing to Šamaš, who will repay him with favour. (W. G. Lambert, *Babylonian Wisdom Literature* [Oxford: Clarendon, 1960], 101, 103).

This advice may be compared with that found in Proverbs 25:21–22 and Romans 12:17–21.

14. Ceslaus Spicq observes, Christ "preserved exactly the spirit of Leviticus which it fulfilled." Ceslaus Spicq, *Agape in the New Testament,* vol. 1, *Agape in the Synoptic Gospels,* trans. M. A. McNamara, M. H. Richter (London: Herder, 1963), 11.

15. Note how this parable follows Jesus' sending out of the seventy-two. Nestled in that account are the words of Luke 10:10–12, in which Jesus directs his

disciples to perform a symbolic curse—a portent of impending doom—against those who do not receive them or their message.

16. Robert Dabney sums up Christ's "law of love" as this:

> The law of love does not require the injured Christian to approve or countenance the evil character manifested in the wrong done him, or to withhold the verdict of truth and justice against it when righteous ends are gained by pronouncing it. The law of love does not require him to intervene for delivering the aggressor from the just claims of either human or divine law for penal retribution; nor does it forbid his feeling a righteous satisfaction when that retribution is executed by the appropriate authorities; but the law of love does forbid his taking retribution into his own hands, and it requires him still to extend the sentiments of humanity and the love of compassion to the enemy's person so long as he continues to partake the forbearance of God, which love of compassion will prompt the injured party to stand ready to forgive the element of personal *damnum* to his enemy, and to perform the offices of benevolence to his person, in spite of his obnoxious character. (Robert L. Dabney, "The Christian's Duty Towards His Enemies," in *Discussions by Robert L. Dabney,* ed. C. R. Vaughan [Richmond: Presbyterian Committee of Publication, 1890], 1:720).

17. Hans Dieter Betz's objection that "such help is directed toward the animals, not toward the enemy" is unwarranted. Hans Dieter Betz, *The Sermon on the Mount,* ed. H. Koester et al. (Minneapolis: Fortress, 1995), 307. In the agricultural milieu of the ancient Near East, these animals were a principal means of support, without which one might easily fall into financial ruin. Although this command positively affects the beast, its intent is primarily to aid the enemy. As the apostle Paul so bluntly asks, obviously expecting a negative response, "Is it about oxen that God is concerned?" (1 Cor. 9:9). Here he speaks not categorically, but for the purpose of emphasis and of divine intent.

18. Paul quotes Proverbs 25:21–22 in Romans 12:20 as an ethical principle. For Old Testament examples that illustrate this command in detail or in principle, see 1 Samuel 24:17; 2 Kings 6:22.

19. Jonah 3–4 demonstrates Yahweh's surprising kindness toward the Assyrians—his inveterate adversaries and the oppressors of his people. In Yahweh's sight, Jonah's behavior was unbecoming when he balked at showing mercy.

20. William Klassen, *Love of Enemies* (Philadelphia: Fortress, 1984), 28. As is repeatedly illustrated in Scripture, love of enemies is shown primarily in deeds of kindness. And this kindness toward enemies (i.e., love in action) *is* commanded in the Old Testament (e.g., Exod. 23:4–5; Prov. 25:21–22).

21. Although Leviticus 19:18 parallels "neighbor" with "one of your people" (i.e., an Israelite), both the near context and the broader Old Testament concept of kindness broke beyond that narrow restriction (cf. Lev. 19:34; Deut. 10:19).

22. Or, "immigrant," a translation of גֵּר (*gēr*) proposed in Frank Anthony Spina, "Israelites as *gērîm*, 'Sojourners,' in Social and Historical Context," in *The Word of the Lord Shall Go Forth: Essays in Honor of David Noel Freedman in Celebration of His Sixtieth Birthday*, ed. C. L. Meyers, M. O'Connor, American Schools of Oriental Research Special Volume Series, ed. E. M. Meyers (Winona Lake, Ind.: Eisenbrauns, 1983), 1:323. Spina notes in his discussion that "immigrants were often viewed as 'enemies' or 'outlaws' in the sense that their attitudes and actions were construed as or in fact constituted an explicit denunciation of the social and political order." Ibid., 328.

23. Cf. Genesis 15:13; Exodus 22:20; 23:9; Deuteronomy 10:19; 23:8; 24:17–22. There appears to be a propensity toward oppression and suspicion against גֵּרִים (*gērîm*). Notice especially Exodus 23:9: "You shall not oppress a stranger [גֵּר, *gēr*]. You yourselves know the soul of a stranger [i.e., how it feels to be one], for you were strangers in Egypt." As Harold Stigers observes, "The clearest sense of the noun *gēr* is seen when used of Israel in their sojourn in Egypt." Harold G. Stigers, "גּוּר," *TWOT*, 1:155.

24. Such a predisposition toward mistreatment belies a latent enmity. In Exodus 23:22–23, God designates the indigenous peoples as enemy nations to be destroyed upon Israel's entrance into Canaan. Deuteronomy 23:4–5 excludes the Moabite from the assembly of Yahweh. Yet Rahab the Canaanite and Ruth the Moabite could be embraced by the community of faith (Josh. 6:25; Ruth 1:16; 4:13–22). King David's stringent measures against the Moabites in 2 Samuel 8:2 may be explained as David's dealing with Moabites as a *nation* as opposed to dealing with them on a personal level. Contrast these drastic

actions with his earlier dependence on the Moabite royalty for their familial loyalty (1 Sam. 22:3–4; cf. Ruth 4:17). In the intervening years, the national enemy of Israel under Saul (1 Sam. 14:47) had become the national enemy of Israel under David. David's relationship with Shobi the Ammonite contrasts with a mortal enmity between David and the kingdom of Ammon under Shobi's brother Hanun (cf. 2 Sam. 10 with 17:27–29).

25. Although not identical to imprecation, a close relationship exists between "woe" and "curse." The cry of woe in the ancient Near East bore a measure of semantic overlap with the curse—and in certain contexts took on "all the characteristics of a curse." Waldemar Janzen, *Mourning Cry and Woe Oracle*, Beiheft zur Zeitschrift für die alttestamentliche Wissenschaft, ed. Georg Fohrer (Berlin: Walter de Gruyter, 1972), 125:3. This is most apparent in Zechariah 11:17, in which an oracle of woe is placed parallel to an evident imprecation:

> Woe to the worthless shepherd,
>> who abandons the flock!
> May the sword strike his arm and his right eye!
>> May his arm be utterly withered,
>> and his right eye utterly blinded!

Compare the curses/woes pronounced against locations of guilt in the Ugaritic Legend of Aqhat:

> Qiru-mayim the king doth *curse:*
>> "Woe to thee, O Qiru-mayim,
> O[n] which rests the blood-guilt of Aqhat the Youth!"
> . . . .
> "Woe to thee, city of Abelim,
>> On which rests the blood-guilt of Aqhat the Youth!
> May Baal make thee blind . . .
>> From now unto all generations!"

James B. Pritchard, ed., *Ancient Near Eastern Texts Relating to the Old Testament*, 3d ed. with supplement (Princeton: Princeton University Press, 1969), 154–55.

Indeed, there is striking similarity not only in mood, but also in form, in content, and in context (cf. Deut. 27:24, "Cursed be he who slays his neighbor in secret!" with Hab. 2:12, "Woe to him who builds a city on bloodshed!"). This similarity between woe and curse is not confined to the Old Testament. The implicitly imprecatory "woe" is found as well in the Sermon on the Plain, in which Christ contrasts his "blessings" with "woes," not the more typical "curses" (Luke 6:20–26). John N. Day, "The Imprecatory Psalms and Christian Ethics" (Ph.D. diss., Dallas Theological Seminary, 2001), 186–190.

26. From the cross, Jesus voices the ultimate expression of enemy-love and of blessing those who persecute and curse. Regarding the ones who had nailed him there, he said, "Father, forgive them, for they do not know what they are doing" (Luke 23:34). Note the creative tension in the differing responses to degrees of enmity shown by the apostle Paul in 2 Timothy 4:14–16. Of Alexander, a hardened enemy of Paul and the gospel, he solemnly states, "The Lord (i.e., Jesus; cf. 4:8) will repay him for what he has done." But concerning those who had wronged Paul by abandoning him in his time of trial and need, he pleads, "May it not be counted against them." The latter expression is reminiscent of the dying words of Jesus in Luke 23:34 and of Stephen in Acts 7:60.

27. For further expressions of imprecation arising out of the context of extremity, see Jeremiah 18:18–23 and Lamentations 3:52–66 (esp. vv. 64–66). In all cases, the basic issues are the same—gross, undeserved enmity, even threatening death, against the pious.

28. In one sense God loves his enemies, and in another he hates them. These complementary reactions are a model for those who follow God's ethical standards, with the understanding in God's people that they also were once enemies of God (Col. 1:21–22).

29. David Alan Black, "The Pauline Love Command: Structure, Style, and Ethics in Romans 12:9–21," *Filologia Neotestamentaria* 2 (1989): 14.

30. Paul apparently had awareness of Christ's sermons, whether or not they had been codified. James D. G. Dunn observes that "the spirit of the Sermon on the Mount breathes through these verses"—particularly noting the influence on Romans 12:14, 17, 19, and 21. James D. G. Dunn, *Romans 9–16*, Word Biblical Commentary, ed. D. A. Hubbard and G. W. Barker (Dallas: Word, 1988), 38B:750–51. Moreover, he avers that "since the contrast between blessing and cursing appears in this form only in Luke 6:28

and Rom. 12:14 (Paul nowhere else uses καταράομαι), the obvious corollary is that the one who provided this decisive moral impetus was Jesus himself, as the Synoptic tradition attests." Ibid., 745. Καταράομαι (*kataraomai*) is the verb meaning "curse."

31. In a section of Scripture dominated by (imperatival) participles, verse 14 stands out starkly in its use of the true imperative and, moreover, shows an apparent dependence on the words of Christ in Matthew 5:44 and Luke 6:28.

32. According to the structure and development of this passage, πονηρόν (*poneron*, "evil; sinful") in verse 9 is synonymous with κακόν (*kakon*, "evil; bad") in verse 21 (cf. its prior introduction in verse 17), both of which function as antonyms of ἀγαθῷ (*agathō*, "good").

33. Black, "Pauline Love Command," 16.

34. Perhaps this is as the Puritan William Gurnall said: "A wicked man cannot wish well to a saint as a saint, as, on the contrary, a saint cannot bless the wicked as such. . . . They do, indeed, desire their conversion, and therein wish them well, but in the wicked way they are in at present they cannot bless them." William Gurnall, *The Christian in Complete Armour* (Glasgow: Blackie & Son, 1864; reprint, Carlisle, Pa.: Banner of Truth, 1974), 2:447.

35. Black, "Pauline Love Command," 18.

36. As C. E. B. Cranfield argues, the force of the ἀπό (*apo*) is intensive. Thus, the term means "to hate utterly." "What is required is not just a refraining from doing what is evil, but an intense inward rejection of it." C. E. B. Cranfield, *A Critical and Exegetical Commentary on the Epistle to the Romans,* International Critical Commentary on the Holy Scriptures of the Old and New Testaments, ed. J. A. Emerton, C. E. B. Cranfield (Edinburgh: T. & T. Clark, 1979), 2:631 n 5. Thomas Schreiner notes that "true virtue is not passive about evil but has an intense revulsion of it. Evil is not tolerated but despised as that which is injurious and wicked." Thomas R. Schreiner, *Romans,* Baker Exegetical Commentary on the New Testament, ed. M. Silva (Grand Rapids: Baker, 1998), 664. Series hereafter cited as BECNT.

37. John Piper, *"Love Your Enemies": Jesus' Love Command in the Synoptic Gospels and in the Early Christian Paraenesis* (Cambridge: Cambridge University Press, 1979), 129–30.

38. Secondarily, the state and the judicial system are to exercise divinely sanctioned vengeance, and the Christian is to uphold that justice and to submit under God to those institutions that exact it (Rom. 13:1–4).

39. Dunn, for one, would assert that these two are irreconcilable, for he views the return of blessing for cursing as a distinctive feature of Christian teaching that constitutes an advance beyond both the more characteristic *lex talionis* attitude of the covenant as previously understood and the more typically Jewish assumption that God would curse those who cursed his people, as promised initially in Genesis 12:3. Dunn, *Romans 9–16*, 744–45.

40. Martin Luther, *Luther's Works*, vol. 21, *The Sermon on the Mount and the Magnificat*, ed. Jaroslav Pelikan, trans. J. Pelikan, A. T. W. Steinhaeuser (St. Louis: Concordia, 1956), 101.

41. E. W. Hengstenberg, *Commentary on the Psalms*, trans. J. Thomson, P. Fairbairn, 4th ed. (Edinburgh: T. & T. Clark, 1869), 3:lxxv.

42. This apparent paradox of the Christian's approach to anger is addressed even in the near context of Ephesians 4:31 cited above; for in verse 26, the command is ostensibly given to "be angry, and sin not"—thus intimating that there is an occasion for righteous indignation, if dealt with properly and swiftly. Cf. Daniel B. Wallace, "ΟΡΓΙΖΕΣΘΕ in Ephesians 4:26: Command or Condition?" *Criswell Theological Review* 3 (1989): 353–72.

Chapter 7: Heaping Coals of Fire

1. *Instruction of Amen-Em-Opet* in James B. Pritchard, ed., *Ancient Near Eastern Texts Relating to the Old Testament*, 3d ed. with supplement (Princeton, N.J.: Princeton University Press, 1969), 422 (emphasis in original). The relevance of this passage to Proverbs 25:21–22 (and its quotation in Rom. 12:20) is borne out in its advice regarding how one is to act toward an enemy: "Treat him with kindness, leaving the matter ultimately to God/the god." *Instruction* bears a similarity to Proverbs 22:17–24:22. It is uncertain, however, whether Proverbs borrowed its common material from Amen-Em-Opet, whether Amen-Em-Opet borrowed from Proverbs, or whether they both drew from a common milieu of wisdom material.

2. Cf. F. L. Griffith, *Stories of the High Priests of Memphis: The Sethon of Herodotus and the Demotic Tales of Khamuas* (Oxford: Clarendon Press, 1900), 32, 38, 121, 135.

3. Siegfried Morenz, "Feurige Kohlen auf dem Haupt," *Theologische Literaturzeitung* 78 (1953): col. 188.

4. William Klassen, "Coals of Fire: Sign of Repentance or Revenge?" *New Testament Studies* 9 (1962–63): 343.

5. Although Proverbs 25:1 indicates that the proverb in question was copied and recorded for posterity by Hezekiah's men, this only advances about two hundred years closer to the Egyptian ritual. It remains five hundred years away. Moreover, the proverb itself is identified as being from Solomon (tenth century B.C.), not Hezekiah (eighth century B.C.).

6. C. E. B. Cranfield is no advocate of this understanding, yet he does relate the fuller position of John Chrysostom, who "explains that Paul knew that even if the enemy were a wild beast he would scarcely go on being an enemy after accepting the gift of food, and that the Christian who has been injured would scarcely go on hankering after vengeance after he has given his enemy food and drink; and [he] goes on to say that to give one's enemy food and drink with the intention of increasing his future punishment would be to be overcome of evil." C. E. B. Cranfield, *A Critical and Exegetical Commentary on the Epistle to the Romans,* International Critical Commentary on the Holy Scriptures of the Old and New Testaments, ed. J. A. Emerton, C. E. B. Cranfield (Edinburgh: T. & T. Clark, 1979), 2:649.

7. Cf. further 2 Esdras 16:53: "God will burn coals of fire on the head of him who says, 'I have not sinned before God and his glory.'" Bruce M. Metzger, ed. *The Oxford Annotated Apocrypha, Revised Standard Version,* expanded ed. (Oxford: Oxford University Press, 1977), 62.

8. The same could be said of Proverbs 25:21–22, whose near context—the additional proverbs of Solomon in 25:1–29:27—does not express a coherent argument. These verses stand alone as their own discrete context. Proverbs 25:21 outlines the general attitude and action of the Old Testament believer toward one's enemy in need. Solomon could have picked up this imagery from its accustomed use in Old Testament literature. He was only a generation after the Davidic psalms 11, 18, and 140, where the image is used. If he did, verse 22 can be interpreted as comfort: The enemy's evil will not go unpunished by the divine Judge, nor will the believer's kindness in the face of enmity go unrewarded. This transaction implies that the hostility of the enemy remains. If this were explained, the statement would lose its conciseness and no longer be a proverb.

9. The primary command is substantiated by two γάρ (*gar,* "for") phrases: *"for it is written, 'Vengeance is mine; I will repay,' says the Lord"* and *"for* in doing

this, you will heap coals of fire upon his head" (emphasis added). This apparently intentional parallel structure suggests strongly that "coals of fire" refers to the same divine eschatological vengeance expressed in verse 19. John Piper, *"Love Your Enemies": Jesus' Love Command in the Synoptic Gospels and in the Early Christian Paraenesis* (Cambridge: Cambridge University Press, 1979), 115. Although the second γάρ is part of the quotation from Proverbs 25:21–22, it functions within that quotation as a word of comfort in support of the actions of kindness. Within the structure of Romans 12:19–20 and the development of its argument, it has a similar function.

10. Krister Stendahl, "Hate, Non-Retaliation, and Love: 1 QS x, 17–20 and Rom. 12:19–21," *Harvard Theological Review* 55 (1962): 354. Stendahl believes it unlikely that "the passage as it stands could reasonably be understood by its first readers in any other sense than as a word related to the vengeance of God." Ibid., 352.

11. Ibid., 354.

12. Piper notes that "there is a very real sense in which the Christian's love of his enemy is grounded in his certainty that God will take vengeance on those who *persist* in the state of enmity toward God's people." Piper, *"Love Your Enemies,"* 118 (emphasis in original).

13. James D. G. Dunn, *Romans 9–16*, Word Biblical Commentary, ed. D. A. Hubbard, G. W. Barker (Dallas: Word, 1988), 38B: 750.

14. Thomas Schreiner makes the summary statement that "the sure realization that God will vindicate us frees us to love others and to do good to them," thus conquering evil with good (Rom. 12:21). Thomas R. Schreiner, *Romans*, BECNT (Grand Rapids: Baker, 1998), 675.

15. Schreiner observes,

> The reference to God's wrath and leaving room for it is exceedingly important in interpreting this text. When we believers are mistreated, abused, and our rights are infringed upon, the desire for retaliation burns within us because we have been treated unjustly. We are not to give in, however, to the desire to get even. Rather, we are to place the fate of our enemies firmly in God's hands, realizing that he will repay any injustice on the last day. . . . Believers are also to pray, of course, that God would bless those who persecute them (Rom. 12:14). This means that we pray for the salvation of our oppressors,

hoping that they will turn from their evil and be rescued from the wrath to come. Nonetheless, we need to know (cf. 2 Thess. 1:3–10 for the same theme) that those who do not repent will experience judgment. (Schreiner, *Romans,* 673–74).

16. Context of the Romans discussion makes it clear that we are not dealing here with issues of "state justice" (e.g., the war on terror and the death sentence for serial murderers, cf. 13:4). The principle of enemy-love does, however, have implications for what Christians should desire. Modern history tells of Christian-promoted efforts to help meet humanitarian needs of current or former enemies. On a personal level, some measure of forgiveness can be extended to criminals in the name of Christ if there is genuine repentance. This does not remove the state's responsibility to execute justice upon the criminal.

17. As Darrell Bock reflects with regard to Christ's love command in the Sermon on the Plain, from which the essence of Paul's remarks in this section was drawn, "The reason the disciple can love all humanity is that the disciple knows that God will deal justly with all one day. Even the woes of Luke 6:24–26 are grounded in God's final act of justice. It is the sermon's eschatology of hope and justice that lays the groundwork for the disciple's love ethic." Darrell L. Bock, *Luke 1:1–9:50,* BECNT, (Grand Rapids: Baker, 1994), 567.

Chapter 8: New Testament Curses

1. This curse was directed both against the fig tree itself and against the nation of Israel, for which the fig tree was a metaphor. What happens to the tree illustrates what will happen to the nation and its sinful leaders. This intimate connection between a symbolic object and what the object signified was common in ancient Near East imprecations.

2. The "days of vengeance" (ἡμέραι ἐκδικήσεως, *hēmerai ekdikēseōs*) referred to in Luke 21:22 reprises Jesus' quotation of Isaiah 61:1–2 in Luke 4:18–19. Judgment against Jerusalem would be "fulfillment of the threat of vengeance (the vengeance of the covenant) made through Moses (in Leviticus 26 and Deuteronomy 32)." Joel Nobel Musvosvi, *Vengeance in the Apocalypse,* Andrews University Seminary Doctoral Dissertation Series (Berrien Springs,

Mich.: Andrews University Press, 1993), 17:137. Musvosvi points out that Jesus does not reject the biblical concept of vengeance in relation to the fig tree any more than in the parable of the widow demanding justice in Luke 18:1–8.

3. This imprecation is indirect but real. The realization of that curse in the life of the nation is more horrible and graphic than anything that would come before or after (Matt. 24:21; Mark 13:19; Luke 21:22–23).

4. Compare the narrative progression in Matthew 21–24, noting especially 21:43: "The kingdom of God will be taken away from you and given to a people who will produce *its fruit*" (emphasis added).

5. Matthew 21:19 has "May you no longer bear fruit—ever!" In Luke's parallel in chapter 19, Jesus speaks of the coming judgment against Jerusalem tearfully and prophetically, but with brutal language: "They will dash [ἐδαφιοῦσιν, *edaphiousin*] you and your children among you to the ground" (v. 44). This recalls Psalm 137:9, in which the LXX uses the same term, ἐδαφιεῖ (*edaphiei*; cf. Hos. 10:14; 13:16).

6. Mark Moulton, "Jesus' Goal for Temple and Tree: A Thematic Revisit of Matt 21:12–22," *Journal of the Evangelical Theological Society* 41 (1998): 564.

7. William L. Lane, *The Gospel of Mark*, NICNT (Grand Rapids: Eerdmans, 1974), 400. Although this action of Christ was indeed a "prophetic sign," it was also an actual imprecation. Indeed, the text calls it a curse and uses curse language. This curse gave assurance of impending calamities to befall the unrepentant people. Indeed, every imprecation in Scripture, if divinely answered, finds its realization in some future action. In this instance, the realization of Christ's imprecation is seen in the ensuing judgment of A.D. 70.

8. The larger context of Mark 11–13 also supports this interpretation. William Hendriksen reasons,

> It is impossible to believe that the curse which the Lord pronounced upon this tree was an act of punishing it, as if the tree as such was responsible for not bearing fruit, and as if, for this reason, Jesus was angry with it. The real explanation lies deeper. The pretentious but barren tree was a fit emblem of Israel. See Luke 13:6–9 (cf. Isa. 5). Jesus himself would interpret the figure the next day. (William Hendriksen, *Exposition of the Gospel According to Mark*, New Testament Commentary [Grand Rapids: Baker, 1975], 442)

9. See the prophetic backdrop to this account in Micah 7:1–4.

10. R. A. Cole, *The Gospel According to Mark: An Introduction and Commentary,* Tyndale New Testament Commentaries, 2d ed. (Leicester, England: Inter-Varsity, 1988), 176–77. Series hereafter cited as TNTC.

11. William R. Telford, *The Barren Temple and the Withered Tree: A Redaction-critical Analysis of the Cursing of the Fig-tree Pericope in Mark's Gospel and Its Relation to the Cleansing of the Temple Tradition,* Journal for the Study of the New Testament—Supplement Series, ed. E. Bammel et al. (Sheffield, England: JSOT, 1980), 1:135 (emphasis in original).

12. Cf. Jeremiah 5:17. Note also that in this context Yahweh asks three times, "Should I not *avenge* myself on such a nation as this?" (vv. 9, 29; 9:8 emphasis added).

13. See how this context repeatedly includes the slaying of Israel's children in the declaration of judgment (Hos. 9:12–14, 16; 10:14; 13:16; cf. Luke 19:44).

14. Since Scripture does record imprecations on the lips of Christ and his apostles, they must have some appropriate place. Christ and the apostles are "types" for Christian life and behavior (e.g., Paul in 1 Cor. 11:1). Occasionally an act may relate strictly to the authority of Christ or his apostles in their persons, ministry, and callings, but those unique apostolic ethics occur relatively infrequently and are easy to discern. Only a few examples of apostolic denunciation can be found, but some are set before us in Scripture. These continue the Old Testament pattern based upon God's promise, models for those who would follow in the footsteps of the first disciples in learning the commands of Christ.

15. The imprecation in 1 Corinthians 16:22 is even broader than that in Galatians 1: "If anyone does not love the Lord, let him be accursed [ἀνάθεμα]!"

16. Johannes Behm, "ἀνάθεμα," *Theological Dictionary of the New Testament,* trans. G. W. Bromiley, ed. G. Kittel (Grand Rapids: Eerdmans, 1964), 1:354.

17. חֵרֶם (*ḥērem*) occurs, for example in Deuteronomy 7:26; 13:17; Joshua 6:17–18; 7:11–15.

18. That the false teachers are not mentioned by name is no proof that Paul approves of only a general curse of damnation. Elsewhere, he does not flinch from naming the apostates and troublers he denounces, such as Alexander in 1 Timothy 1:20; 2 Timothy 4:14, and Elymas in Acts 13:10–11.

19. Cf. I. Howard Marshall, *The Acts of the Apostles,* TNTC (Leicester: Inter-Varsity, 1983), 159. The language of Peter is explicitly imprecatory, but his

intent is to threaten, as evidenced by his call for repentance. Thus, in the mind of Peter—and in certain other scriptural imprecations—there is an evident blending between the two domains of curse and threat. In their usage they often overlap and inform each other.

20. Derek Kidner, *Psalms 1–72*, Tyndale Old Testament Commentaries, ed. D. J. Wiseman (London: Inter-Varsity, 1973), 30.

21. Such is the understanding of Paul's words for Joseph Fitzmyer, among others: "Paul curses Bar-Jesus and, in effect, calls upon the Lord to cause the blindness." He adds, "The curse that Paul has laid on the magician is instantaneous in its effect." Joseph A. Fitzmyer, *The Acts of the Apostles*, Anchor Bible, ed. W. F. Albright, D. N. Freedman (New York: Doubleday, 1998), 31: 503. Although given in the future tense as a proclamation of judgment, it nonetheless bears the essence of a curse, for it is uttered as the express wish of Paul (a wish immediately fulfilled). Moreover, it conforms to the pattern revealed, for instance, in Deuteronomy 28:15ff., in which promises of judgment are given as the "curses" of the covenant.

22. Compare the result of Paul's curse on Elymas ("Immediately mistiness and darkness fell upon him, and he groped about, seeking someone to lead him by the hand," Acts 13:11), with Deuteronomy 28:28–29 ("Yahweh will smite you with . . . blindness. . . . You will grope about at midday like a blind man gropes about in the darkness."). Blindness was a common curse-theme in the ancient Near East, as can be seen from the vassal-treaties of Esarhaddon: "May Shamash . . . take away your eyesight; walk about in darkness!" James B. Pritchard, ed., *Ancient Near Eastern Texts Relating to the Old Testament*, 3d ed. with supplement (Princeton, N.J.: Princeton University Press, 1969), 538.

23. That blindness is the punishment sets a parallel between this curse and the temporary blindness of Paul's conversion experience. That the curse was to remain in effect "for a time," indicates that the curse was intended to leave the door open to repentance and restoration.

24. John Calvin, *Commentary upon the Acts of the Apostles*, first published 1560, trans. C. Fetherstone, 1585, ed. Henry Beveridge (Edinburgh: Calvin Translation Society, 1844), 1:508. Calvin further admits and argues, "Neither am I ignorant how easily men may fall in this point; for which cause godly teachers must take so much the more heed, first, that they favour not the affections of the flesh too much under the colour of zeal; secondly, that

they break not out with headlong and unseasonable heat where there is yet place for moderation; thirdly, that they give not themselves over to foolish and uncomely railing, but only that they express the unseemliness of the thing by gravity and weight of words. Such was the vehemency of holy zeal and of the Spirit in the prophets, which if dainty and soft men judge troublesome and raging, they consider not how dear and precious God's truth is to him." Ibid., 509.

25. William Klassen, "'Love Your Enemies': Some Reflections on the Current Status of Research," in *The Love of Enemy and Nonretaliation in the New Testament,* ed. W. M. Swartley (Louisville: Westminster John Knox, 1992), 21.

26. John Calvin, *Commentaries on the Epistles of Paul to the Galatians and Ephesians,* trans. W. Pringle (ET, Grand Rapids: Eerdmans, 1948), 157.

27. Musvosvi, *Vengeance in the Apocalypse,* 158. The call for vengeance justly follows the shedding of innocent blood. Ibid., 185. Moreover, this call for vengeance to the Master [ὁ δεσπότης, *ho despotēs*] "is to be understood in the light of the covenant motif, wherein the suzerain is obligated to bring redress and justice when a vassal is attacked and injured" (p. 216). The death of the martyrs is viewed in Revelation 6:9 as a "sacrifice," given that the souls have their place "under the altar" (cf. Lev. 17:11 and 4:7ff., "the soul/life of the flesh is in the blood," poured out "at the base of the altar").

28. G. K. Beale notes that the expression "how long?" is used throughout the Greek Old Testament—notably in the Psalms—for questions concerning when God will finally punish persecutors and vindicate the oppressed. G. K. Beale, *The Book of Revelation,* New International Greek Testament Commentary, ed. I. H. Marshall, D. A. Hagner (Grand Rapids: Eerdmans, 1999), 392. This prayer follows a pattern seen among imprecatory psalms (e.g., Pss. 74:10–11; 79:5–6, 10, 12; 94:1–3). In the martyrs' cry there is an understood petition "to carry out vengeance against those who have shed that blood." Robert L. Thomas, *Revelation 1–7: An Exegetical Commentary,* Wycliffe Exegetical Commentary, ed. K. Barker (Chicago: Moody, 1992), 445–46. Every appeal to God for harm to justly fall on wicked persons is an imprecatory prayer.

29. The essential mood of Psalm 94 is similar to that of other imprecatory psalms. The cry for vengeance is founded on the complaint: "They crush your people, O Yahweh, and they oppress your inheritance! They slay the widow and the sojourner, and they murder the fatherless!" (vv. 5–6).

30. Robert L. Thomas, "The Imprecatory Prayers of the Apocalypse," *Bibliotheca Sacra* 126 (1969): 130.
31. Context indicates that these martyrs were "ordinary" believers, who were killed when they stood up for Christ. Such an imprecatory prayer from representative Christians and recorded from a heavenly vantage point, offers strong assurance that this petition is not wrong.
32. Notably in Revelation 15:3, the principal concern is the coming of promised divine vengeance. This vengeance is central to the latter part of the Song of Moses (Deut. 32). The book of Revelation skillfully binds this Song to the Song of the Lamb. As the book progresses to its climax, it is the slain Lamb who returns as divine Avenger (cf. Rev. 5 and 19).

Conclusion

1. The imprecatory psalms as a class are characterized by entreaty for ill to befall enemies of God and his people. These entreaties may be expressed in a direct or indirect appeal for divine vengeance.
2. James Adams contends that "when these holy prayers are again prayed in the Spirit and with understanding, there will come unsuspected power and glory to the church of Christ." James E. Adams, *War Psalms of the Prince of Peace: Lessons from the Imprecatory Psalms* (Phillipsburg, N.J.: Presbyterian & Reformed, 1991), xiii. Likewise, Walter Brueggemann expresses the purpose in his work to "contribute to the vitality of the church's faith by pointing to the subversive and powerful resources available in the Psalms. It is an unreformed church that uses the Psalms for a domesticated spirituality. It is not an accident that the Reformers of the sixteenth century attended to the Psalms in intensive ways." Walter Brueggemann, *Praying the Psalms* (Winona, Minn.: Saint Mary's, 1986), 10. Moreover, the imprecatory psalms include curses against both individuals and corporate enemies. Applying these psalms to modern life will include both spheres as well.
3. Reflecting on the implications inherent in the Lord's Prayer, oft repeated in corporate and individual worship, Johannes Vos argues that the church must again learn to embrace the mislaid truth that "God's kingdom cannot come without Satan's kingdom being destroyed. God's will cannot be done in earth without the destruction of evil. Evil cannot be destroyed without the destruction of men who are permanently identified with it." Johannes G.

Vos, "The Ethical Problem of the Imprecatory Psalms," *Westminster Theological Journal* 4 (1942): 138.

4. Edwards noted with dismay—even in his day—that there was "such a protrusion of the promises of the Bible, and such a concealment of its threatenings, as to neutralize the influence of both. Religion is sometimes so divested of its grander and sterner qualities as to fail to secure any respect. It becomes a mere collection of pleasant counsels, an assemblage of sweet recommendations, which it would be very well to observe; instead of presenting, as it does, an alternative of life and death, an authoritative code of morals, a law with inflexible sanctions, a gospel to be rejected on peril of eternal damnation." B. B. Edwards, "The Imprecations in the Scriptures," *Bibliotheca Sacra* 1 (1844): 109–10.

Appendix: Responding to Severe Persecution

1. This sermon was preached by the author at Bellewood Presbyterian Church (PCA) in Bellevue, Washington on November 10, 2002. International Day of Prayer for the Persecuted Church has been sponsored each November since 1996 by World Evangelical Fellowship (WEF).

2. Adapted from testimony in "The Voice of the Martyrs" newsletter, November 2001.

Bibliography

Abusch, Tzvi. "An Early Form of the Witchcraft Ritual *Maqlû* and the Origin of a Babylonian Magical Ceremony." In *Lingering over Words: Studies in Ancient Near Eastern Literature in Honor of William L. Moran,* ed. T. Abusch, J. Huehnergard, P. Steinkeller, 1–57. Atlanta: Scholars Press, 1990.

————. "The Demonic Image of the Witch in Standard Babylonian Literature: The Reworking of Popular Conceptions by Learned Exorcists." In *Religion, Science, and Magic: In Concert and In Conflict,* ed. J. Neusner, E. S. Frerichs, P. V. McCracken Flesher, 27–58. New York: Oxford University Press, 1989.

Adams, James E. *War Psalms of the Prince of Peace: Lessons from the Imprecatory Psalms.* Phillipsburg, N.J.: Presbyterian & Reformed, 1991.

Adamson, James B. *The Epistle of James.* New International Commentary on the New Testament, ed. F. F. Bruce. Grand Rapids: Eerdmans, 1979.

Aland, Barbara; Kurt Aland; Johannes Karavidopoulos; Carlo M. Martini; and Bruce M. Metzger, eds. *The Greek New Testament.* 4th rev. ed. Stuttgart: Deutsche Bibelgesellschaft, 1994.

Allen, Leslie C. *Psalms 101–150.* Word Biblical Commentary, ed. D. A. Hubbard, G. W. Barker. Waco, Tex.: Word, 1983.

Althann, R. "The Psalms of Vengeance Against Their Ancient Near Eastern Background." *Journal of Northwest Semitic Languages* 18 (1992): 1–11.

Augustine. *Saint Augustine: Expositions on the Book of Psalms,* ed. A. C. Coxe. A Select Library of the Nicene and Post-Nicene Fathers of the Christian Church, ed. P. Schaff; trans. J. E. Tweed, T. Scratton, H. M. Wilkins, C. Marriott, H. Walford. New York: Charles Scribner's Sons, 1917.

Barnes, Albert. *Notes, Critical, Explanatory, and Practical, on the Book of Psalms.* New York: Harper & Brothers, 1868.

Beale, G. K. *The Book of Revelation.* New International Greek Testament Commentary, ed. I. H. Marshall, D. A. Hagner. Grand Rapids: Eerdmans, 1999.

Beardslee, J. W. "The Imprecatory Element in the Psalms." *Presbyterian and Reformed Review* 8 (1897): 490–505.

Betz, Hans Dieter. *The Sermon on the Mount,* ed. A. Yarbro Collins. Hermeneia, ed. H. Koester et al. Minneapolis: Fortress, 1995.

Black, David Alan. "The Pauline Love Command: Structure, Style, and Ethics in Romans 12:9–21." *Filologia Neotestamentaria* 2 (1989): 3–22.

Blank, Sheldon H. "The Curse, Blasphemy, the Spell, and the Oath." *Hebrew Union College Annual* 23 (1950–51): 73–95.

Bock, Darrell L. *Luke 1:1–9:50.* Baker Exegetical Commentary on the New Testament, ed. M. Silva. Grand Rapids: Baker, 1994.

———. *Luke 9:51–24:53.* Baker Exegetical Commentary on the New Testament, ed. M. Silva. Grand Rapids: Baker, 1996.

Bonhoeffer, Dietrich. "A Bonhoeffer Sermon." Ed. F. B. Nelson; trans. D. Bloesch. *Theology Today* 38 (1982): 465–71.

———. *Psalms: The Prayer Book of the Bible.* Trans. J. H. Burtness. Minneapolis: Augsburg, 1970.

Brichto, Herbert Chanan. *The Problem of "Curse" in the Hebrew Bible.* Journal of Biblical Literature Monograph Series. Vol. 13. Philadelphia: Society of Biblical Literature, 1968.

Bright, John. *The Authority of the Old Testament.* Nashville: Abingdon, 1967.

Brueggemann, Walter. *Praying the Psalms.* Winona, Minn.: Saint Mary's, 1986.

———. *The Message of the Psalms: A Theological Commentary.* Minneapolis: Augsburg, 1984.

Bush, L. Rush. "Does God Inspire Imprecation? Divine Authority and

Ethics in the Psalms." Evangelical Philosophical Society Presidential Address, November 16, 1990.

Calvin, John. *Commentaries on the Epistles of Paul to the Galatians and Ephesians.* Trans. W. Pringle. Reprint, Grand Rapids: Eerdmans, 1948.

———. *Commentaries on the Epistles to Timothy, Titus, and Philemon.* Trans. W. Pringle. Reprint, Grand Rapids: Eerdmans, 1948.

———. *Commentary on the Book of Psalms.* Vol. 2. Trans. J. Anderson. Edinburgh: Edinburgh Printing, 1846. Reprint, Grand Rapids: Baker, 1979.

———. *Commentary on the Book of Psalms.* Vol. 4. Trans. J. Anderson. Edinburgh: Edinburgh Printing, 1847.

———. *Commentary upon the Acts of the Apostles.* Ed. H. Beveridge; trans. C. Fetherstone, 1585. Edinburgh: Calvin Translation Society, 1844.

Carson, D. A. *The Sermon on the Mount: An Evangelical Exposition of Matthew 5–7.* Grand Rapids: Baker, 1978.

Charlesworth, James H., ed. *The Dead Sea Scrolls: Hebrew, Aramaic, and Greek Texts with English Translations.* Vol. 1, *Rule of the Community and Related Documents.* Louisville: Westminster John Knox, 1994.

Cole, R. A. *The Gospel According to St. Mark.* Tyndale New Testament Commentaries, ed. R. V. G. Tasker. Leicester, England: Inter-Varsity, 1988.

Craigie, Peter C. *Psalms 1–50.* Word Biblical Commentary, ed. D. A. Hubbard and G. W. Barker. Waco, Tex.: Word, 1983.

———. *The Book of Deuteronomy.* New International Commentary on the Old Testament, ed. R. K. Harrison. Grand Rapids: Eerdmans, 1976.

Cranfield, C. E. B. *A Critical and Exegetical Commentary on the Epistle to the Romans.* International Critical Commentary on the Holy Scriptures of the Old and New Testaments, ed. J. A. Emerton and C. E. B. Cranfield. Edinburgh: T. & T. Clark, 1979.

Crawford, Timothy G. *Blessing and Curse in Syro-Palestinian Inscriptions of the Iron Age.* American University Studies: Series 7, Theology and Religion, vol. 120. New York: Peter Lang, 1992.

Dabney, Robert L. "The Christian's Duty Towards His Enemies." In *Discussions by Robert L. Dabney,* ed. C. R. Vaughan, 706–21. Vol. 1. Richmond: Presbyterian Committee of Publication, 1890.

Day, John N. "The Imprecatory Psalms and Christian Ethics." Ph.D. diss., Dallas Theological Seminary, 2001.

Driver, S. R. *A Critical and Exegetical Commentary on Deuteronomy.* 3d
    ed. International Critical Commentary on the Holy Scriptures of the
    Old and New Testaments, ed. Samuel Rolles Driver et al. N.p., 1902.
    Reprint, Edinburgh: T. & T. Clark, 1965.
Dunn, James D. G. *Romans 9–16.* Word Biblical Commentary, ed. D. A.
    Hubbard, G. W. Barker. Dallas: Word, 1988.
Edwards, B. B. "The Imprecations in the Scriptures." *Bibliotheca Sacra* 1
    (1844): 97–110.
Elliger, K., and W. Rudolph, eds. *Biblia hebraica stuttgartensia.* Stuttgart:
    Deutsche Bibelgesellschaft, 1983.
Fensham, F. Charles. "Common Trends in Curses of the Near Eastern
    Treaties and *Kudurru*-Inscriptions Compared with Maledictions of
    Amos and Isaiah." *Zeitschrift für die alttestamentliche Wissenschaft*
    75 (1963): 155–75.
Fitzmyer, Joseph A. *The Acts of the Apostles.* Anchor Bible, ed. W. F.
    Albright, D. N. Freedman. New York: Doubleday, 1998.
———. "The Aramaic Inscriptions of Sefire I and II." *Journal of the Ameri-
    can Oriental Society* 81 (1961): 178–222.
Gevirtz, Stanley. "Curse Motifs in the Old Testament and in the Ancient
    Near East." Ph.D. diss., University of Chicago, 1959.
———. "West-Semitic Curses and the Problem of the Origins of
    Hebrew Law." *Vetus Testamentum* 11 (1961): 137–58.
Gibson, John C. L. *Textbook of Syrian Semitic Inscriptions.* Vol. 1, *Hebrew
    and Moabite Inscriptions.* Oxford: Clarendon, 1971.
Gilbert, Bobby J. "An Exegetical and Theological Study of Psalm 137."
    Th.M. thesis, Dallas Theological Seminary, 1981.
Greenfield, Jonas C., and Aaron Shaffer. "Notes on the Curse Formulae
    of the Tell Fekherye Inscription." *Revue biblique* 92 (1985): 47–59.
Griffith, F. L. *Stories of the High Priests of Memphis: The Sethon of Herodotus
    and the Demotic Tales of Khamuas.* Oxford: Clarendon, 1900.
Guillaume, Alfred. "The Meaning of תולל in Psalm 137³." *Journal of Bibli-
    cal Literature* 75 (1956): 143–44.
Gunkel, Hermann. *What Remains of the Old Testament and Other Essays.*
    Trans. A. K. Dallas. London: Allen & Unwin, 1928.
Gunn, George S. *God in the Psalms.* Edinburgh: Saint Andrew Press, 1956.
Gurnall, William. *The Christian in Complete Armour; A Treatise of the*

Saints' War against the Devil: wherein a Discovery is made of that grand Enemy of God and his people, in his Policies, Power, Seat of his Empire, Wickedness, and chief design he hath against the saints. A Magazine Opened, From whence the Christian is furnished with Spiritual Arms for the Battle, helped on with his Armour, and taught the use of his Weapon: together with the happy issue of the whole War. Vol. 2. Glasgow: Blackie & Son, 1864. Reprint, Carlisle, Pa.: Banner of Truth Trust, 1974.

Hammond, Joseph. "An Apology for the Vindictive Psalm (Psalm cix)." *Expositor* 2 (1875): 325–60.

————. "The Vindictive Psalms Vindicated." Introductory–Part 4. *Expositor* 3 (1876): 27–47; 101–18; 185–203; 452–71.

Harman, Allan M. "The Continuity of the Covenant Curses in the Imprecations of the Psalter." *Reformed Theological Review* 54 (1995): 65–72.

Hendriksen, William. *Exposition of the Gospel According to Mark.* New Testament Commentary. Grand Rapids: Baker, 1975.

Hengstenberg, E. W. *Commentary on the Psalms.* Vol. 3. 4th ed. Trans. J. Thomson, P. Fairbairn. Edinburgh: T. & T. Clark, 1869.

Hibbard, F. G. *The Psalms Chronologically Arranged, with Historical Introductions; and a General Introduction to the Whole Book.* 5th ed. New York: Carlton & Porter, 1856.

Hillers, Delbert R. *Treaty-Curses and the Old Testament Prophets.* Biblica et orientalia. Vol. 16. Rome: Pontifical Biblical Institute, 1964.

Janzen, Waldemar. *Mourning Cry and Woe Oracle.* Beiheft zur Zeitschrift für die alttestamentliche Wissenschaft, ed. G. Fohrer. Vol. 125. Berlin: Walter de Gruyter, 1972.

Keil, C. F., and F. Delitzsch. *The Pentateuch.* Trans. J. Martin. Biblical Commentary on the Old Testament. Vol. 3. Edinburgh: T. & T. Clark, 1866. Reprint, Grand Rapids: Eerdmans, 1963.

Kidner, Derek. *Psalms.* 2 vols. Tyndale Old Testament Commentaries, ed. D. J. Wiseman. London: Inter-Varsity, 1973, 1975.

Klassen, William. "Coals of Fire: Sign of Repentance or Revenge?" *New Testament Studies* 9 (1962–63): 337–50.

————. *Love of Enemies.* Philadelphia: Fortress, 1984.

————. "'Love Your Enemies': Some Reflections on the Current Status of Research." In *The Love of Enemy and Nonretaliation in the New Testament*, ed. W. M. Swartley, 1–31. Louisville: Westminster John Knox, 1992.

Kline, Meredith G. *The Structure of Biblical Authority*. Grand Rapids: Eerdmans, 1972.

Kraus, Hans-Joachim. *Psalms*. 2 vols. Trans. H. C. Oswald. Minneapolis: Augsburg, 1988, 1989.

———. *Theology of the Psalms*. Trans. K. Crim. Minneapolis: Augsburg, 1986.

Lambert, W. G. *Babylonian Wisdom Literature*. Oxford: Clarendon, 1960.

Lane, William L. *The Gospel of Mark*. New International Commentary on the New Testament, ed. F. F. Bruce. Grand Rapids: Eerdmans, 1974.

Laney, J. Carl. "A Fresh Look at the Imprecatory Psalms." *Bibliotheca Sacra* 138 (1981): 35–45.

Lewis, C. S. *Christian Reflections*, ed. W. Hooper. Grand Rapids: Eerdmans, 1967.

———. *Reflections on the Psalms*. New York: Harcourt, Brace, 1958.

Longman, Tremper, III. *How to Read the Psalms*. Downers Grove, Ill.: InterVarsity, 1988.

Luther, Martin. *Luther's Works*. Vol. 21, *The Sermon on the Mount and the Magnificat*. Ed. J. Pelikan; trans. J. Pelikan and A. T. W. Steinhaeuser. St. Louis: Concordia, 1956.

Marshall, I. Howard. *The Acts of the Apostles*. Tyndale New Testament Commentaries, ed. R. V. G. Tasker. Leicester: Inter-Varsity, 1983.

Martin, Chalmers. "The Imprecations in the Psalms." *Princeton Theological Review* 1 (1903): 537–53.

McCarthy, Dennis J. *Treaty and Covenant: A Study in Form in the Ancient Oriental Documents and in the Old Testament*. Rome: Biblical Institute Press, 1978.

McKenzie, John L. "The Imprecations of the Psalter." *American Ecclesiastical Review* 111 (1944): 81–96.

Meier, Gerhard. *Die assyrische Beschwörungssammlung Maqlû*. Berlin: Archiv für Orientforschung, Beiheft 2, 1937.

Mennega, Harry. "The Ethical Problem of the Imprecatory Psalms." Th.M. thesis, Westminster Theological Seminary, 1959.

Mercer, Samuel A. B. "The Malediction in Cuneiform Inscriptions." *Journal of the American Oriental Society* 34 (1914): 282–309.

Metzger, Bruce M., ed. *The Oxford Annotated Apocrypha, Revised Standard Version.* Exp. ed. Oxford: Oxford University Press, 1977.

Morenz, Siegfried. "Feurige Kohlen auf dem Haupt." *Theologische Literaturzeitung* 78 (1953): cols. 187–92.

Moulton, Mark. "Jesus' Goal for Temple and Tree: A Thematic Revisit of Matt 21:12–22." *Journal of the Evangelical Theological Society* 41 (1998): 561–92.

Mowinckel, Sigmund. *The Psalms in Israel's Worship.* 2 vols. Trans. D. R. Ap-Thomas. Nashville: Abingdon, 1967.

Musvosvi, Joel Nobel. *Vengeance in the Apocalypse.* Andrews University Seminary Doctoral Dissertation Series. Vol. 17. Berrien Springs, Mich.: Andrews University Press, 1993.

Osgood, Howard. "Dashing the Little Ones Against the Rock." *Princeton Theological Review* 1 (1903): 23–37.

Peels, H. G. L. *The Vengeance of God: The Meaning of the Root* NQM *and the Function of the* NQM-*Texts in the Context of Divine Revelation in the Old Testament.* Oudtestamentische Studiën, ed. A. S. Van der Woude. Vol. 31. Leiden: E. J. Brill, 1995.

Piper, John. *"Love Your Enemies": Jesus' Love Command in the Synoptic Gospels and in the Early Christian Paraenesis.* Cambridge: Cambridge University Press, 1979.

———. *The Pleasures of God: Meditations on God's Delight in Being God.* Portland, Ore.: Multnomah, 1991.

Pritchard, James B., ed. *Ancient Near Eastern Texts Relating to the Old Testament.* 3d ed. with supplement. Princeton, N.J.: Princeton University Press, 1969.

Rahlfs, Alfred, ed. *Psalmi cum Odis.* 3d ed. *Septuaginta: Vetus Testamentum Graecum.* Vol. 10. Göttingen: Vandenhoeck & Ruprecht, 1979.

Reiner, Erica. *Šurpu: A Collection of Sumerian and Akkadian Incantations.* Graz: Archiv für Orientforschung, Beiheft 11, 1958.

Schreiner, Thomas R. *Romans.* Baker Exegetical Commentary on the New Testament, ed. M. Silva. Grand Rapids: Baker, 1998.

Spicq, Ceslaus. *Agape in the New Testament.* Vol. 1, *Agape in the Synoptic Gospels.* Trans. M. A. McNamara, M. H. Richter. London: Herder, 1963.

Spina, Frank Anthony. "Israelites as *gērîm*, 'Sojourners,' in Social and Historical Context." In *The Word of the Lord Shall Go Forth: Essays in*

Honor of David Noel Freedman in Celebration of His Sixtieth Birthday, ed. C. L. Meyers, M. O'Connor. ASOR Special Volume Series, ed. E. M. Meyers, 1:321–35. Winona Lake, Ind.: Eisenbrauns, 1983.

Spurgeon, C. H. *The Treasury of David: Psalms 104–118.* Vol. 5. New York: Funk & Wagnalls, 1881.

———. *The Treasury of David: Psalms 125–150.* Vol. 7. New York: Funk & Wagnalls, 1886.

Stendahl, Krister. "Hate, Non-Retaliation, and Love: 1 QS x, 17–20 and Rom. 12:19–21." *Harvard Theological Review* 55 (1962): 343–55.

Surburg, Raymond F. "The Interpretation of the Imprecatory Psalms." *Springfielder* 39 (1975): 88–102.

Sutcliffe, E. F. "Hatred at Qumran." *Revue de Qumran* 2 (1960): 345–56.

Sutherland, Kandy Maria Queen. "The Futility Curse in the Old Testament." Ph.D. diss., Southern Baptist Theological Seminary, 1982.

Swartzback, Raymond H. "A Biblical Study of the Word 'Vengeance.'" *Interpretation* 6 (1952): 451–57.

Telford, William R. *The Barren Temple and the Withered Tree: A Redaction-critical Analysis of the Cursing of the Fig-tree Pericope in Mark's Gospel and Its Relation to the Cleansing of the Temple Tradition.* Journal for the Study of the New Testament—Supplement Series, ed. Ernst Bammel et al. Vol. 1. Sheffield: JSOT Press, 1980.

Teigen, Ragnar C. "Can Anything Good Come From a Curse?" *Lutheran Quarterly* 26 (1974): 44–51.

Theological Dictionary of the New Testament. Translated by Geoffrey W. Bromiley. Ed. Gerhard Kittel. Vol. 1. Grand Rapids: Eerdmans, 1964.

Theological Dictionary of the Old Testament. Translated by John T. Willis. Ed. G. Johannes Botterweck and Helmer Ringgren. Vol. 1. Revised ed. Grand Rapids: Eerdmans, 1977.

Theological Wordbook of the Old Testament. Edited by R. Laird Harris, Gleason L. Archer Jr., and Bruce K. Waltke. 2 vols. Chicago: Moody, 1980.

Thomas, Robert L. "The Imprecatory Prayers of the Apocalypse." *Bibliotheca Sacra* 126 (1969): 123–31.

———. *Revelation 1–7: An Exegetical Commentary.* Wycliffe Exegetical Commentary, ed. Kenneth Barker. Chicago: Moody, 1992.

Thompson, R. Campbell. *The Devils and Evil Spirits of Babylonia.* Vol. 1. London: Luzac & Company, 1903. Reprint, New York: AMS Press, 1976.

Thrupp, Joseph Francis. *An Introduction to the Study and Use of the Psalms.*
Vol. 2. Cambridge: Macmillan, 1860.

Ulrich, Eugene, et al. *Qumran Cave 4, IX: Deuteronomy, Joshua, Judges, Kings.* Discoveries in the Judean Desert. Vol. 14. Oxford: Clarendon, 1995.

The Voice of the Martyrs newsletter, November 2001.

Vos, Johannes G. "The Ethical Problem of the Imprecatory Psalms." *Westminster Theological Journal* 4 (1942): 123–38.

Wallace, Daniel B. "ΟΡΓΓ ΖΕΣΘΕ in Ephesians 4:26: Command or Condition?" *Criswell Theological Review* 3 (1989): 353–72.

Walton, John H. *Ancient Israelite Literature in Its Cultural Context.* Grand Rapids: Zondervan, 1989.

Webb, William J. "Bashing Babies Against the Rocks: A Redemptive-Movement Approach to the Imprecatory Psalms." Unpub. presentation, Evangelical Theological Society, November 2003.

Weiser, Artur. *The Psalms.* Trans. H. Hartwell. Old Testament Library, ed. G. E. Wright et al. Philadelphia: Westminster, 1962.

Wenham, Gordon J. *The Book of Leviticus.* New International Commentary on the Old Testament, ed. R. K. Harrison. Grand Rapids: Eerdmans, 1979.

Wenham, John W. *The Goodness of God.* Downers Grove, Ill.: InterVarsity, 1974.

Wevers, John William, ed. *Deuteronomium. Septuaginta: Vetus Testamentum Graecum.* Vol. 3.2. Göttingen: Vandenhoeck & Ruprecht, 1977.

White, R. E. O. *A Christian Handbook to the Psalms.* Grand Rapids: Eerdmans, 1984.

Wiseman, D. J. *The Vassal-Treaties of Esarhaddon.* London: British School of Archaeology in Iraq, 1958.

Wright, David P. "Blown Away Like a Bramble: The Dynamics of Analogy in Psalm 58." *Revue biblique* 103 (1996): 213–36.

———. "Ritual Analogy in Psalm 109." *Journal of Biblical Literature* 113 (1994): 385–404.

Wright, G. Ernest. "The Lawsuit of God: A Form-Critical Study of Deuteronomy 32." In *Israel's Prophetic Heritage: Essays in Honor of James Muilenburg,* ed. B. W. Anderson, W. Harrelson, 26–67. New York: Harper & Brothers, 1962.

Zenger, Erich. *A God of Vengeance? Understanding the Psalms of Divine Wrath.* Trans. L. M. Maloney. Louisville: Westminster John Knox, 1996.

Zuck, Roy Ben. "The Problem of the Imprecatory Psalms." Th.M. thesis, Dallas Theological Seminary, 1957.

Scripture Index

APOCRYPHA

Subject Index

abortion 55, 148–49n. 19
Abraham, cursing of 160n. 24; as father of the church 129n. 37. *See also* covenant, Abrahamic.
Adams, James E. 33, 55, 139n. 70, 148–49n. 19, 178n. 2
Adamson, James B. 148n. 18
Al Qaeda 72
Alexander, denunciation of 67, 82, 138n. 68, 167n. 26, 175n. 18
Allen, Leslie C. 71–72, 157n. 14
Althann, Robert 133–34n. 35
Ammon 166n. 24
anathema 104
anger 92; being "slow to anger" 92; paradox of the Christian approach to 169n. 42
Antichrist 72
Aqhat, Legend of 167
Assyrian vassal treaties 38–39
Augustine 94–95, 152n. 8

Babylon 64, 69, 151–52n. 2, 154nn. 25, 26; Revelation view of 60, 67, 70; 155n. 31
Balaam 145n. 38, 159n. 23
bārû 145n. 38
Beale, G. K. 177n. 28
Beardslee, J. W. 125n. 21

Betz, Hans Dieter 165n. 17
Bin Laden 72
Black, David Alan 90–91
Blank, Sheldon H. 144n. 38
blessing and cursing 90–92, 113, 114
blindness, curse of 142n. 12, 176n. 22
Bock, Darrell L. 172–73n. 17
Bonhoeffer, Dietrich 33–34, 55, 139n. 80
Brichto, Herbert Chanan 45
Bright, John 63
Brueggemann, Walter 25, 82, 161n. 34, 178n. 2
Bush, L. R. 131n. 13

Calvin, John 54, 75–76, 105, 106, 137–38n. 61, 147n. 8, 156n. 4, 176n. 24
Carson, D. A. 85
Christians, hostility against 9
Chrysostom, John 95–96, 170n. 5
"coals of fire" metaphor 93–94, 114, 171n. 9
Cole, R. Alan 102
condemnation 157n. 14
Counsels of Wisdom 163–64n. 13
courts and judges in Psalms 155n. 31, 158n. 18
covenant 10, 109, 120–21; Abrahamic 30–31, 56, 122; blessing of 13, 25, 79–81, 110, 113, 137n. 52; faith

196